FINANCIAL LITERACY

FOR YOUNG ADULTS

End Your Money Problems and Reach Financial Independence at a Young Age with Brilliant Budgeting, Profitable Investing and Smart Money Management

EMILY CARTER

YOUR FREE GIFT

To really make the most out of your life, and to succeed in it, it's crucial to never stop learning. To further develop your knowledge of important life skills, I've got something for you… something you can really be excited about!

As a way of saying thank you for your purchase, I want to offer you some BONUSES completely FREE of charge:

To get instant access, just go to:

<https://lifeskillbooks.com>

Here's just a glimpse of what is included:

BONUS 1

91 Easy Ways to Save Money This Year:
Practical Steps for Smarter Spending

Inside this checklist, you will discover...

- Surprisingly simple ways to start saving money already today!

- The Clever Money-Saving Techniques for shopping that you most likely have not discovered yet.

- And much more! 91 tips in total. That's a lot.

BONUS 2

101 Fast Fixes to Boost Your Credit Score:
Your 101-Step Roadmap to Credit Success

Inside this 71-page!! ebook, you will discover...

- Gain a solid understanding of the fundamentals of credit scores and how they impact your financial health, setting the stage for informed decision-making.

- Identify common mistakes that can negatively impact your credit score, some of which you are most likely doing yourself!

- And finally... learn to build a perfect credit score for yourself, even if you're starting from the bottom.

BONUS 3

Automated Money Management Playbook: Simplified Guide to Hands-Off Financial Management

Inside this useful playbook, you will discover...

- The benefits of automated finances and why you should start automating your finances already today.

- The 7 Must-have tools for seamless automation.

- Invaluable tips and tricks for automating all your transactions from paying bills to retirement investing and everything in between.

Now, go visit the website below for instant access to these three and several other amazing bonuses. Completely free of charge.

https://lifeskillbooks.com

TABLE OF CONTENTS

INTRODUCTION

*"I believe that through knowledge
and discipline, financial peace is
possible for all of us."*

Dave Ramsey.

You, too, can have it all – true, it sounds like a cliché from a commercial! But really, do you think you have what it takes to have it all?

I have been thinking a lot about how to begin this introduction, and I discovered that honesty always works best. So, I'm going to be honest with you. I am someone who has spent a lot of time, especially during my young adult years not really knowing how to handle finances. I was constantly struggling and reading books on the topic, but it seemed like something was missing.

Then I realized what that something was – I kept trying to blindly follow everyone else's experiences and how they handled money instead of finding a way that would work for me. Granted, it took me a little longer than expected to reach this point, but right after I did, I realized that everything I've ever learned about finances is finally making sense.

So, I began working – I did my best, invested, made safe (and a little risky) financial choices, and came up with multiple income sources. It sounds like a dream, doesn't it? Well, in the middle of it all, I found that I was losing my balance. It's not my actual balance (I can keep that), but my work-life balance. Suddenly, it felt like I was right there where I started. It was like I did a full circle and returned to the beginning. I felt discouraged and, again, thought that I didn't know where to begin. That's when something in my mind just clicked.

Financial literacy doesn't require a background in algebra or business – it requires a strong mindset and determination. It requires a little bit of persistence and some strategies, so you know you're making the logical financial steps. Once I implemented this behavior into my life, everything started making sense once more.

The beauty of finance is that you learn things about the world and society, but mostly yourself, with each passing day. It is also about gaining experience in what matters most to you.

The thing is, not a lot of people believe this. And I understand where you're coming from. As a young adult, you are currently at a crossroads – you want to achieve as much as you can in life. You know you can accomplish a lot, but you are also baffled by all the options out there, and the more options you have, the more confused you get. It seems like you cannot find the proper balance, and even if you do, you still have this overwhelming feeling that you're doing something wrong.

Well, I am here to tell you that all's well that ends well. You do not need to panic anymore or feel like you're letting yourself down because, through this book, you will learn all there is to know about finances. As you go through this book, you will notice that financial literacy includes a lot of different aspects, such as interest rates, pensions, loans, etc. To make things as clear and concise for you, I have added plenty of examples – after all, we all learn through examples in life, right?

You are embarking on a journey that will lead you straight to the gates of financial independence and security. Through it, you will learn about recognizing the importance of saving and spending, how to earn money, identify good and bad debt, and how to plan ahead. Even if a part of you thinks that you cannot learn all of this, I can assure you that after you read this book, you will emerge as a new, improved, and financially literate you.

So don't be afraid to turn the first page! I know there is at least a little excitement within you, just waiting to burst into flames. That will happen as soon as you learn everything I've outlined in these pages.

Forget everything you've seen until now. This book will provide you with a bullet-proof way of understanding money, looking at money, and handling money.

From one financial sprout to another – you got this!

MINDSET

*"Make sure you have financial intelligence...
I don't care if you have money, or you don't have
money... you need to go, and study
finance no matter what."*

Daymond John

The most difficult thing you will encounter on your way to financial independence and success is getting into the right mindset. Up until this point in your life, you have probably relied on your parents or guardians to give you the financial stability you need. But the wheel never stops turning, our caregivers grow old, and we are the ones responsible for our own faith.

Picture this scenario – you finish high school; you go to college (or any other educational institution) and it is time for you to become an independent person. All of which sounds great – having the liberty to be who you want to be and do what you want to do, but one thing is constantly on your mind – *what about your finances?*

Whether you know that this stage in your life is fast approaching, or you've already reached it, learning how to get into the right financial mindset takes time. It is a challenging process, but it is also a rewarding one.

Financial literacy and mindset are not taught in schools. With that in mind, we can start our journey to educate you about the most important topics connected to finances – which will be the foundation of everything you do in the future.

Understanding the mindset required for financial success

A mindset is your belief and your attitude toward the world around you, how you perceive it, and how you respond to it. It is the glasses through which you see your life opportunities, challenges, and setbacks.

Cultivating a strong mindset starts with understanding how it affects your finances. A weak mindset will not result in financial success, but a strong one just might. Your mindset affects not only what you think but also what you do and how you make decisions. Do you approach finances with hesitation or determination? It's time to learn about the mindset you need for financial success.

Fixed or growing?

Nobody explains the difference between the fixed and the growth mindset better than Carol Dweck. She studies human motivation, and her research on this topic is exactly what you need to start your journey. In her study, the difference the two mindsets make in outcomes is extremely powerful. Some people succeed, and others don't (depending on their mindset). She explains how your view of yourself determines everything in life.

If you believe you are born with a specific set of qualities and think they cannot change, then you have a fixed mindset. The opposite of that is learning from your mistakes. In her words, "The hand you're dealt with in life is just the starting point for development." That's what a growth mindset looks like - and it is exactly what you need to begin your journey to financial stability, literacy, and independence.

Having a growth mindset means focusing on the most important aspects of becoming more successful and independent. By accepting this approach, you will be able to shift, learn, and progress every single time. This is exactly what you need to fight (or go with) the ever-changing currents of money. It is what will help you grow and re-discover your powers over and over again.

With that in mind, here are the most important financial aspects where you need to put your growth mindset to use if you want to achieve financial success.

Financial challenges

These are something all of us have had at some point in life. However, when you come face to face with financial challenges, it is crucial to know how to deal with them head-on. Setbacks in life happen – that's when you return to the previous point. A fixed mindset will lead you to defeat and constant fear, despair, and helplessness. Contrary to that, the growth mindset will enable you to see that current situation as an opportunity for growth and development.

Financial Education

As much as you have avoided this in the past, it is time to face the fact – financial education is a must. Learning about finances is a long-term process, one you should invest in every time you can. By continuously expanding your financial knowledge, you invest in yourself and your ability to tackle finances successfully.

Financial decisions

Another aspect where your mindset plays an important role is that a strong growth mindset can help you approach financial decisions with confidence, while a fixed mindset will keep whispering in your ear that you're making a mistake. If you have a fixed mindset, that does not mean you're fixed in one place. You can always switch to the growth mindset, no matter how long it takes. Accepting the fact that you get a valuable learning experience each time you make a financial decision is a step in the right direction.

Financial resilience

As I mentioned earlier, financial setbacks happen – but that doesn't mean you should think it is the end of the world. That leads us to the final point – financial resilience. Investing wisely, saving wisely, and having enough to weather the financial storms that may come your way is essential. A strong mindset can help you remain focused on achieving your goals. Once you have a clear roadmap, it can help you overcome challenging situations.

Developing a long-term perspective

The growth mindset may seem like an unattainable goal at this point. The reality is that anyone can reach it. There are a few practices you should consider on your way to shift your mindset entirely, and the first one is developing a long-term perspective. By doing so, you will start looking at your status quo objectively and working toward a better financial tomorrow.

Developing a long-term perspective is a process that encompasses the following steps:

1. Evaluate your current situation

When you are creating a long-term perspective about your finances, you need to look at your current financial position. This includes your cash flow, net worth, liabilities, expenses, assets, income, and credit score. Once you gather and organize the information, see how much you save, spend, and invest. By tracking your movements, you can identify your weaknesses and strengths and even issues you need to address in the future.

2. Write down clear goals

Having a long-term objective is a crucial part of the process, but you need to be clear and concise about it. Every one of us wants to achieve something with the money we make, and if you are honest with yourself, you will get the most specific answer out of you. Be specific and write down a clear goal. For example – instead of saying, "I want to save money," say, "I want to save (a specific amount) for (a specific purpose) in (a specific timeframe)." For example, "I want to save $20,000 for a down payment on a house in two years."

3. Develop a strategy

The next step is to take action. If you want to achieve your financial goals, it is only logical that you develop a strategy that will bring you closer to your objectives with each passing day. Consider a few options, check how much you need to invest, spend, and save. Then, consider whether you are willing to take some risks. Create a timeline for each goal and track your progress regularly.

4. Review your assumptions

The long-term financial plan consists of estimates and expectations too. You should base these assumptions on your current situation, goals, strategies, and objectives. Before proceeding in a new direction, ensure the premises are realistic and consistent with the current market climate. Incorporate a few different scenarios into the assumptions and closely monitor the outcomes. Doing this will help you identify all the opportunities, errors, gaps, and other aspects that may affect your long-term financial stability.

5. Adjust accordingly

A part of a growth mindset is learning how to bend to future outcomes – sometimes, you will need to take a different path from the one you initially set and accepting that fact helps you get closer to achieving your goals. You may find that some significant changes will amend your current trajectory, and it is important to consider them into the equation and constantly adjust accordingly. This can be anything from changes in your personal or professional life to changes in taxes, interest rates, and inflation. Always focus on being flexible and adapting to the new conditions with ease – as long as they still reflect your long-term goals.

6. Seek assistance

This is something you have already done by reading this book! Financial stability and success come from knowledge, and it is always a good idea to seek advice on this topic. By doing this, you can take some solid financial steps and implement everything you've learned to draft the perfect long-term financial plan. Getting some valuable information, insights, recommendations, and resources is what can take your entire planning to the next stage.

The compound effect

The Compound Effect is a book by Darren Hardy that has significantly changed the way I view and approach finances. The core of this book lies in taking small actions that align with your long-term goals. It focuses on always taking full responsibility for what happens to you and underlines the importance of measuring something before you start changing it.

Let's talk about this a bit. Why is this book so important that we are discussing it here?

There's a thin line between your mindset and what you achieve. To that extent, what you believe in is what you achieve. Think of it as the ultimate power of self-observation. It is about having a real conversation with yourself. Because the compound effect is a system that is running your life, whether you are aware of it or not, this goes unnoticed in most people's lives.

But the reality of the situation is that you are your own creator. You are in charge of your own life, and the sooner you realize that; the sooner you can take some steps to create a better, financially successful version of yourself.

Making the right decision is something you choose every day, from when you wake up to when you go back to sleep. These small decisions you make, the small steps you take – all of them shape your destiny – who you are and who you will become. To implement it into the business and finances aspect of your life, you create a small operating system based on your abilities, the funds available to you at the moment, and your goals. Making a success scheme is only the beginning. Your progress may not be visible to you, but once you reach the first, second, or even third milestone and look back on what you've created, you will see that your desire to live an extraordinary life filled with abundance and richness is happening.

The compound effect is a strategy through which you accumulate a certain amount of wealth by making some small, almost insignificant steps every day. Through time, if you stay consistent and make small choices that benefit you, you end up reaping the fruits of your labour - financial success.

Picture this - what would happen if you made a scheme as mentioned just now, and be 1% better, or give 1% more every day? What would happen to you already in one year? On the contrary, what would happen if you gave 1% less and less with each passing day?

Allow me to show the math: If you improve yourself by 1% every single day for 365 days (one year) in a row, you will end up being 37.8 times better than you were when you started. That is a 3780% increase! And let me tell you, that's a lot. On the contrary, if you were to be 1% worse or less each passing day, after a year you would end up being only 3% of what you were when you started.

Here's a very simple real-life example - with a physical workout. When you want to get better or give a little bit more every day in terms of exercising, you will not see the difference immediately (of course, nobody does). However, if you try to push yourself each day - with one more push-up, or one more lunge, or deadlift, by the time one year has passed, you will be unrecognizable.

The thing is, you will also be unrecognizable a year from now if you give less and less every day. If you start doing less than you should, and ultimately you quit working out, the results will be more than evident. Actually, they will be more than evident either way. What's left of you is to discover which way you will go.

The compound effect is best described this way. No matter how much you give, as long as it is more, it piles up on top of one another and multiplies until you reach a point where you have an abundance to enjoy.

The basics of the compound effect are in the growth mindset. As long as you adhere to that and to the points we have gone over in this chapter, there is no way to remain in the same situation you are in right now. At all times, remember that even the smallest actions you take, the ones you think are the least significant to your being and your professional life, matter a lot.

I can only hope that you have gained some insight into what you need to start creating your financial independence today. To give you a little reminder, review the summary below.

What did you learn from this chapter?

- What is your mindset, and how it can help you achieve financial success?
- The difference between a fixed and a growth mindset.
- The most important financial aspects for success.
- How to develop a long-term perspective (and stick to it).
- What is the compound effect, and the beauty of incorporating it into your financial planning.

As we close this chapter and look into the future, you might still find yourself on the edge about "what's about to happen." Even if your mind wonders about whether the worst-case scenario will come true or not, this book is designed to put all your negative thoughts about it to rest. It is also intended to answer the easiest and most challenging questions you didn't think to ask.

In the next chapter, we will talk about how to prepare yourself for "rainy days."

WEATHERING THE STORM - PREPARE YOUR EMERGENCY FUND

"Tough times never last, but tough people do."

Robert H. Schuller

We only touched upon this topic in the previous chapter, so now it is time to open it and see what hides beneath the surface. No matter how young or financially inexperienced you are, you have probably noticed by now that everyone faces an economically difficult period at some point in their lives. The fundamental principle that can help you escape it (should you face it yourself) is to remain calm, collected, and ready to take action. Yes, being financially unstable can indeed make you feel overwhelmed and even make you panic at times, but it is essential to let go of that so you can focus on what you can control – and ultimately change. These difficult times have always been temporary, and as the quote at the beginning of this chapter says – only tough people last. So, let's see what you can do to make the most out of this situation.

Now, you are going to learn all about planning. It is not just about working hard to achieve your goals – it is about being smart about them, determined about what you want, and giving yourself the time to turn around any financial situation you stumble into.

The importance of emergency funds and their role in financial security

Life has always been filled with surprises, and if there is one thing you can learn from, you should always have a "secret stash." What does that mean? The importance of having an emergency fund is often overlooked, but if you want optimal financial well-being, it is a must. It is kind of like a safety net, something that will keep you from falling on the ground and spiralling down about what you're going to do now. Having financial security gives you peace of mind.

So, what is an emergency fund?

Life is unpredictable, and everything can change in the blink of an eye. Of course, no need to get into a worst-case scenario right now, but you probably see where I'm going with this. Unforeseen expenses happen all the time. When these things happen, you must be prepared – this is when the emergency fund kicks in.

The emergency fund represents a stash of money you have put aside for emergencies and unexpected events. This indicates that you are safe no matter what happens to you, even when life throws you the biggest curveballs.

Why is the emergency fund so important?

There are a few reasons why having an emergency fund is so important:

- You are financially secure in case of an emergency.

- You are protected in case of a reduction in income or loss of a job.

- You can cover all sorts of expenses (whether it is medical bills, car bills, home repairs, or anything else).

- You get to be independent and confident in your financial choices.

- You avoid getting into debt.

- You can support both yourself and a loved one, a relative, or a friend.

- You have the opportunity to seize an unexpected investment or business opportunity.

- You are flexible and able to handle any disruptions in income.

- You are prepared for anything that comes your way – whether it is to achieve your future aspirations or experience some sort of an accident.

How to build an emergency fund?

All this talk about having an emergency fund made you think – how can you create your own fund? Take a look at the steps below.

1. Set a goal – The goal-setting part is crucial because you cannot create an emergency fund without it. To have a good financial backup plan, first, you need to choose how much you want to save. Many experts on this subject have said that a stash of three to six months of living expenses is an average amount. This includes rent, bills, groceries, and every other necessary expense.

    But this is not always the case, so you need to take a look at your unique current situation. You can start creating a target based on your circumstances and comfort level. You might end up having to save less than you expected yet still have enough to call your savings an emergency fund. Just remember, the goal is to cover your basic needs if necessary.

2. Automating your savings – having a goal is one thing, but automating your savings is probably the best way to achieve that goal. When you view savings as substantial as paying your bills or buying groceries for the month, you will save the money you want much faster than expected. If possible, you can set up automatic transfers from your paycheck every month.

    It is the beauty of the "set it and forget it" approach. With little to no effort, you will create an incredible emergency fund. It can be a percentage of your paycheck, a fixed amount – anything you like – as long as it gets you started.

3. Cut back on expenses – and save the money instead. Creating an emergency fund requires a lot of discipline. It takes dedication, effort, and determination. You should be willing to change your spending habits. When you take a closer look at what you are spending on a weekly or monthly basis – make a detailed view of it, you can easily find something to cut back on. Some of the costs may be completely unnecessary, and even if they are the slightest changes, they can still make an impact.

    Don't fret over this one – no need to make drastic changes. It can be anything from changing your streaming service subscription, gym membership, anything, really! Notice the unnecessary expenses and take it from there.

4. Contribute more – this means that, at some point, you are bound to get some extra cash flow – it can be a tax return, a bonus from work, or an extra project you've taken on. Take

these funds and add them to your emergency fund. The extra contribution you make will go a long way when needed.

The reality is that you don't really need the money at the moment, so why not save it? It is still there, and you can still reach it anytime you want. Doing this adds an extra layer of financial safety to your life. Also, it gives you the opportunity to reach your emergency fund goals a lot faster.

While I talked about emergency fund being the foundation of your financial security, another thing you have probably already heard of might have already come to your mind - insurance. That is good, since insurance is an incredibly important part of financial security too. But what do you think of when you think of insurance? Do you imagine some sort of a safety net? Or do you believe it has something to do with life insurance, car insurance, etc? You are right either way. Before we move on to understanding financial risks, let's talk a bit about insurance.

Insurances

Sometimes, life happens, and this is the sole reason why people turn to insurance. We are not powerful against the grand forces, and unexpected things can happen at any turn. When, and if this happens, you need to know that you have something to fall back on. That's where the insurance kicks in.

So far, the word insurance is something you have probably associated with your parents or guardians, and you thought it was a "grown-up" topic. However, since you are entering your early adult years, you need to immediately focus on it so you can build a safer financial future on top of it.

There is a certain importance to having insurance in your life, and being insured is a part of being an adult. As an inexperienced party, it is okay to wonder where to begin. I know that insurance is not the most thrilling subject to talk about, but you should always have something to fall back on. While there are different types of insurance, some of them are very common, and an advised choice for young adults. This is where things get interesting. The types of insurance vary, and the ones below are ones you should strongly consider having.

1. Health insurance - this should be on the top of your list. If we take America into consideration, most people there need insurance to afford healthcare. Do your research so you can choose the right option for yourself. Why is this important? Because it will be the first thing you fall back on if you come face to face with medical debt. Fun fact - a lot of people in America get health insurance through their employer or their spouse's employer - and these people usually don't need extra insurance. Another fun fact - you can stay on your parents' health insurance up until the age of 26.

2. Auto insurance - this is for all of you who own a car. Even a small fender bender can cost a lot, and having auto insurance will ensure you have all the potential damage to the vehicle and bodily harm covered. The auto insurance varies from one model to the next, as well as the living location, your age, your credit score, and your driving record. You will need this all throughout your life, up until the point you stop driving a car.

3. Renters insurance - in case you are renting out an apartment, consider renters insurance. If you live by yourself or on a college campus - you need renters insurance. Just like with auto insurance, this also varies depending on the location, the coverage amount, and the type of home, but it is usually

of a very low cost. In turn, it covers the replacement of personal property in case of an unwelcoming situation, and a temporary living place if you are unable to live in the home you've rented.

4. Disability insurance - this is something that will provide you with insurance in case you are unable to work. Relying on a steady paycheck or working toward something more, something you've created yourself can take a toll on your overall health. In any case, you don't know what the future has in store for you, and the disability insurance is there in case something happens to you.

5. Life insurance - what you've probably heard the most - in movies, in series, in real life - life insurance is the talk of the town, every time. The reason why this is happening is because at some point in life, someone else may rely on your income for their financial well-being. Since life insurance is so common, it is cheap, and the right policy depends on your overall financial situation. How much you pay, how much risk you pose, and what type of policy you get will determine the coverage. You will stop needing it when your dependents no longer rely on you for financial support.

6. Homeowners insurance - as soon as you become a homeowner, you will need to get homeowners insurance because it covers anything from your personal belongings to the structure itself, to liability if someone is injured on your property. The homeowner's insurance depends on the location, size, and age of the building. For example, if you live in an area that is more prone to wildlife or tornados, you might need more premium insurance. As soon as you stop being a homeowner and sell your home, you will stop needing this type of insurance too.

7. Pet insurance - last but not least, this is the kind of insurance that you will probably consider - but it has never crossed your mind until now. Being a young adult, you might have a pet by your side, and whatever that may be (a dog, a cat, a parrot) you need to insure them too - after all, they are sort of your property, right? Should anything happen to them, you should be prepared. From a routine vaccination and vet visits to urgent surgery, this type of insurance will cover up to 90% of your bills.

Considering insurance before you move on to understanding and managing financial risks is what will help you create a more solid plan. Now let's talk about risks!

Understanding and managing financial risks

Becoming a part of modern financial society means knowing what risk and risk management mean. This knowledge can enable you to develop resilience when times get tough.

In its broader terms, a financial risk represents the possibility of losing money on an investment. The results can be minor or major losses depending on the risk. This casts such a wide net that it serves both businesses and individuals. The dangers that may come with a financial risk are mostly related to odds. If this happens, you may be unable to satisfy your most basic needs.

While there are financial risks for businesses, governments, and markets, there are also individual financial risks – which will be the central point of our learning.

Everything from highly speculative investments to taking days off of work without a particular purpose may be a financial risk for you. As you go deeper into the topic of finances when reading this book, you will notice one thing – you are always 100% responsible for your own actions – nobody else can take responsibility for you. That is why, every time you take a step, you need to assess the risks and the potential consequences.

The dangers of financial risk may be beyond our control sometimes. How can that happen? Depending on where you have put your focus of attention, three main things can "go wrong."

1. If you are dealing with assets and market liquidity happens, you can either be at a loss or not able to sell or purchase something at a reasonable rate – proceeding with that kind of transaction may only result in a loss.

2. You may be at a loss of funding. When you are employed, things can change in the blink of an eye. Nobody is ever really safe. Sometimes, the company you work for may be forced to cut down on its spending because it doesn't have enough capital to pay off everybody.

3. Which leads us to the third thing - accidents. These things are by far the most out of your control, and they can come in various forms - personal accidents, or any other type of accident that may prevent you from being a fully functional part of the workforce may result in loss of cash flow.

Thankfully, while some things are out of your control, others aren't. Your finances can undergo a strategy where you can always be prepared for the unexpected. It is time to learn the basic methods of risk management. Their beauty is that you can apply them to every aspect of your life (even though we're only talking about finances here.) In the long run, these can help you apply yourself much better in financial situations and always come out on top.

Think of personal financial risk management as an invisible obstacle you need to be prepared for, should it become visible at some point in your life. Because it can be quite challenging to overcome once you come face to face with it, it is better to come prepared, right? Before you go into actual strategies that can help you make the most out of your risk management, let's talk a little bit about why you are doing it in the first place.

You're doing it for financial security. At the end of the day, everyone wants to be financially stable and independent. A part of risk management means focusing on having some backup. That is why it is important to focus on creating a solid emergency fund, having essential insurance, and learning how to deal with debt. Because you will know how to take better action once you realize where you're going with your strategy (what your end goal is).

To elaborate even more on the topic, here are some risk management strategies you can incorporate into your life:

1. Avoidance – avoid some financial activities that do not make you feel safe. For example, if you want to focus on your emergency fund and want to fill it up as fast as possible, why not remove some activity that doesn't contribute to the overall quality of your life? You can lower your alcohol or cigarette consumption and make a difference in more than one aspect of your life. You may feel better almost immediately.

2. Retention – this part is all about accepting a risk as it is given. Usually, this happens when you want to offset some larger risk down the road, such as health insurance for example. The more basic plan comes with a higher deductible rate. In this case, you are at risk of paying more from your pocket should any medical expenses arise, but what is the chance

of that happening? As this is a unique situation for everybody, assess yours before you act accordingly.

3. Sharing – this happens when you share the risk with somebody (often an employer). For example, they will share premium health insurance with you, and both parties will participate in the insurance benefits. This comes from the logic that the more people share it, the more the insurance costs will come down. Some people find this to be in their best interest.

4. Transferring – for example, when you want to insure your car, the risk is transferred from the individual and the car (that's you) to the insurer. As soon as you decide to create and sign a contract with an insurance company, the document will clearly state that some conditions have to be met. In this case, when those conditions are not met, the insurer is the one who takes complete financial responsibility.

5. Prevention and reduction – there are many ways for you to try to minimize your losses. As you can see, this is a pretty extensive list, with prevention and reduction as the last point. This method will not completely eliminate the risk but will only minimize it. In this case, you accept the risk but are focused on containing the loss and preventing it from worsening. Spotting potential issues in your initial plan can help you minimize your losses – naturally, if you act fast.

Moving as far away as possible from debt means always being prepared with an emergency fund. As you noticed, in this chapter we elaborated on all kinds of safety nets you can turn to - and you realised that whatever you do - it is a smart move for your future.

What did you learn from this chapter?

- That even though difficult times never last, you still need to know how to weather the storm.

- What is an emergency fund, why it is crucial, and how to create it.

- You learned about the most common types of insurance and learned that you need it in every stage of your life.

- What is risk management?

- Why and how are you at a financial risk?

- How can you shield yourself from it?

Once you learn the importance of emergency funds and risk management, it is time to explore some more exciting topics! While this was incredibly important, the next few chapters will teach you exactly how to make your financial dream of stability come true. In the following chapter, we will dissect the topic of budgeting. I bet you can't wait for this one!

CHAPTER 3

BUDGETING AND SETTING FINANCIAL GOALS

"A budget tells us what we can't afford, but it doesn't keep us from buying it."

William Feather.

The fundamental aspect of becoming a grown-up is learning how to make and manage finances. When reality hits, most young adults are baffled and still trying to decide which direction to proceed. What we learned is that, in some cases, young people take personal finance courses after graduating high school. This is an excellent starting point for all those who want to learn all about budgeting.

But when this is not the case, how can you possibly know how to manage your finances properly? You could try. However, it might feel like a part is missing, like you could do more and do better.

This chapter is all about that – the knowledge to manage money is one of the most powerful things you can learn. It is time to learn the basic financial rules that can help you build a stable and healthy financial future.

Fundamentals of budgeting

By now, you have probably already heard about the importance of budgeting. It is one of the most crucial aspects of gaining financial freedom, and for a good reason – budgeting can help you become more stable in your management and create better long-term financial stability.

Before we delve any deeper, let's start with the most basic use – what is budgeting, and why do we use it? Budgeting is a known financial tool that can help you determine how much you spend daily, weekly or monthly vs how much you earn. People use budgeting as an approach to set realistic financial goals. It is the reason why everyone uses it – by budgeting, you can evaluate exactly how you spend and save your money and whether that aligns with your priorities or not.

When you start your budgeting, it is essential to realize that there are different budgeting methods, and after looking into these types, you should choose one that works best for you. Your budgeting success depends on finding an approach that works specifically for you. With that in mind, here are the three most common types of budgeting:

1. Traditional budgeting

This approach organizes spending into categories based on their expense type (fixed or variable expense*) and allows for a certain amount of money for each category. For example, when you have your fixed expenses ready, you make a plan for how much to spend on your variables depending on the day-to-day needs. Once you reach your limit, either put the rest in your savings account or simply stop spending for that month.

Fixed expenses are the ones that stay the same every month and do not change, such as rent, property taxes, loan payments, insurance, etc. Variable expenses are those that change from one month to the next, and these include groceries, utilities, entertainment, clothing, travel, commuting, etc.

2. Reverse budgeting

This type of budgeting is also known as "paying yourself first" because it prioritizes savings above all else. Instead of focusing on your spending, you focus on allocating the money that is at the top of your priority list and then go down the list. For example, if your goal is to save a certain amount of money and set your monthly savings to reach it, you do that first. Then, you turn to your fixed expenses and, finally, to your variable expenses. If you happen to run out of money somewhere along the way, revisit your plan to make the necessary adjustments – after all, you can't allow yourself to run out of money entirely, right?

3. Zero-based budgeting

This type seems like a pretty reasonable approach to many (especially those who are new to the subject of financial stability). Zero-based budgeting means allocating all of your income to specific functions – expenses, savings, donations, debt, and ensuring nothing is left before your next monthly income. With this system, you should reach "ground zero" by the time the month is up.

Practical steps for creating and sticking to a budget

The budgeting types may all seem easy on paper, but when it is time for you to start using them, things can easily go awry. That's why financial experts over the years have created a solid plan filled with practical steps – to help you create and stick to your budget. Taking the best steps and advice throughout the years helped create the best approach, as shown below. It will help you keep your finances in check, prepare for your future, and achieve all your financial goals.

- Track how much you spend. As a young adult, maybe tracking how much you spend on a night out is not the first thing on your mind. Well, it should be. In order to make a solid plan, you must understand where you spend your money first. Any type of tracking will do – a spreadsheet, a notebook, an app on your phone – as long as you manage to categorize your transactions. That will give you a sense of where you spend all the money you earn. There is no need to categorize them from the beginning; this is all about getting the bigger picture before you go into details.

- Prioritize your fixed expenses. You need to successfully manage your fixed expenses to improve your financial future and reach your goals. Whether it is a higher rent rate, a debt you need to pay off, or an insurance you want to maintain, setting aside enough to manage your fixed expenses will give you the stability you need. Instead of spending your hard-earned income on variable expenses of all kinds, taking care of your fixed expenses first gives you the freedom to focus on your goals.

- Set goals. These can be both short-term and long-term goals. Doing this is a great way to keep track of your financial success. It is a way for you to "keep your eyes on the prize." Remember, if you don't know where to begin, always start by writing things down – and start small. For example, you can dedicate an entire section to your short-term goals (let's say on a weekly basis) and work toward achieving them. Even the most minor practices, such as these, will significantly impact your financial stability and long-term success rate.

- Always go into detail. The best way to make a successful financial plan that will lead you to a happier future is to create a plan right down to the last detail. As such, this financial plan will help you assess your current position, identify what you want to achieve in the future and create a map of how to achieve them. You have all the freedom and control here. You can choose to go down any road – now that you know all the budgeting types, you just need to begin.

- The 50/30/20 budget. This is a very popular approach that many young people use. It has even helped me become a more responsible adult and is an easy concept to adhere to. It is all about splitting your income. Use 50% of your income to cover all the essentials (this includes both fixed and variable expenses such as rent and groceries). Use the 30% to buy yourself something you want that month (this part can be reserved for clothing, travel expenses, etc). Finally, use the last 20% to put aside – these will be your monthly savings. Once you start sticking to this simple rule of dividing your monthly income, you can easily budget your spending without removing some fun purchases you want to make that month.

- Dedicate a journal. As mentioned earlier (and it will be mentioned a few times more in this book.) Having a place where you keep all your notes and expenses is important, especially at the beginning of your budgeting journey. Doing this can help you organize your goals, your spending, your savings, and the time you dedicate to achieving your financial freedom. There is no right or wrong way of doing it. Just by writing things down, you are using a helpful method that will help you organize your life better.

- Keep your taxes in the back of your mind. Always keep your taxes in mind. The amount on your salary is not the exact amount that reaches your account. That is why a part of the planning process is using your monthly income after you've put aside the tax money. Do your research and see if you are eligible for tax deductions. If the answer is yes, you might reach some of your financial goals sooner than expected, (such as creating your emergency fund).

- There is also something called the envelope method. While you have probably not heard it until now, many people know it as a popular budgeting method that can help you control your expenses. The envelope method uses a few envelopes (of course). In each of these envelopes, you dedicate a certain amount of money you're allowed to spend for that particular cause. Take groceries as an example – it is something you spend money on every month, but the amount changes all the time. This way, you can make a partially fixed expense out of a variable expense, which is an excellent approach to managing your money. For one month, dedicate a certain amount of your income to groceries and put that money in the envelope. Sticking to the amount you've set aside for that purpose can help you avoid overspending. Doing this gives you a physical sense of the money, and you may take much better care of it by putting it to use every month.

- Control your savings by letting go of controlling them. In other words – automate your savings. This is another good practical tip that can help you start your budget. Since it was mentioned before, it means that it is a pretty solid step you can take. Instead of having your budgeting plan change every month, automate your savings by setting up automatic transfers. You have full control over the sum you want to put aside, and this money is automatically taken from your account when your paycheck arrives. It is mainly viewed as an effortless way of saving since you don't have to think over it – the money practically saves itself!

Setting achievable and realistic financial goals

As you read this chapter, the first thing you will probably stick to the most is the previous part, filled with practical steps on how to create a budget. But, when it comes to budgeting, you can't make a budget if you fail to include the financial goals you have. Starting to outline them means paving the way for your future - knowing how to set realistic and achievable goals means reaching financial maturity.

You've been trying so hard to achieve your financial goals. You've done everything and adhered to all the steps, some of you have even taken a side hustle to achieve your goals. However, when the end of the month comes, something is still missing – and that's usually the amount of money you were supposed to save.

In today's world, things like inflation and recession can be a solid excuse for why you can't save. You may even try to make an excuse by claiming that the above-mentioned practical steps don't work in real life. But we both know neither is the case.

Setting achievable and realistic goals is about wanting to make progress with your money – you're not just saying that; it is something you genuinely wish to achieve. Many people make the mistake of sticking to a certain financial approach without having any financial goals in the first place. So now, we are taking a step back and learning all there is to know about financial goals before going to the next chapter at full speed!

You probably set goals for every aspect of your life. The same should go for finances. Setting a financial goal means knowing what you want to do with your money (having a plan for it.) This goal makes you committed. But, if you want to achieve lifelong success, then you need to prioritize. That's where this book comes in handy! Your reality is this – a lot of things can influence what you think and how you set specific financial goals. They depend on your dreams for the future, your spending habits, your income, and how well you handle money. It takes a lot to handle your goals and make them as specific as possible. That's why you should look into the actionable steps below – I bet they will greatly help you.

1. Start by putting yourself as a priority. There is a reason why this is the first step of the process - you need to be calm, centered, and ready to take on the challenge that is your financial stability. When you decide the only person, you want to work on is yourself, everything else will start falling into place.

2. When you focus on your goals, writing them down is what will help you get a sense of them. There is something about putting things, "pen to paper" as they say that fully validates the intent of the goals - it makes them stronger, it makes them real, and it helps you stay committed.

   Also, while you write down your goals, make them as specific as possible. One of the main reasons why people don't succeed in their quest to reach their goals is because their goals are not specific enough. Instead of being vague, be as specific as possible. For example, if you are looking to build up a good safety net of financials stored in the bank, don't say that to yourself – be specific! Write the exact amount you want to have in your savings account. That makes the goal measurable, too, not just specific. You can almost touch it. You can write them in your journal, on your phone, on a Post-it, on a piece of paper, etc., and take them anywhere you go. There is something about this that will make you work harder than before.

3. Make a deadline. Now, this may put a little bit of pressure on some of you who have been more than eager to reach your goals and be the boost you need from others. Either way, it is okay. As long as you approach this as a challenge you know you can overcome, you will eventually stop saying, "I will be one day," and will start saying, "I already began." A deadline will give you another dimension to make your financial goal setting feel more real.

4. Ensure yourself they are your goals, not someone else's. Sometimes, we all get influenced – by the people around us, society, tradition, and current standards of what is acceptable and what isn't. This can happen without you ever noticing it - so check the goals with yourself before you set them in stone. However difficult it may be, you need to be completely truthful to yourself as you write down the goals. Are these financial goals yours, or are you simply creating goals just to "catch up with the people around you?" If you are not in the same place as some people around you, that's okay. It doesn't mean that you are not in a good place if you're not there alongside them. Stay in your lane, and always ensure the goals you write down and set out to achieve are yours completely and uniquely.

5. Get a buddy. With that in mind, every person needs a little help regarding accountability. To take your entire financial planning a step further, you need to find a so-called accountability buddy. This could be anyone – a friend, a relative, your partner – anyone who can cheer you on your journey and check on you to see if you're still going on the right path. They can help you out whenever times get tough. Also, you will immediately notice the difference in your journey. It means a lot to have someone stand by you, while you work on achieving your financial goals.

Budgeting is a process where you will keep going back and forth - but knowing that taking a step back doesn't mean retreating, but rather trying to look at the bigger picture is what this subject is all about. By determining your financial goals and taking the practical steps to achieve them you will create the foundation of your financial freedom.

What did you learn from this chapter?

- You learned what budgeting is.

- You discovered the three most common types of budgeting, each explaining how it can assist you in achieving your goals.

- Sticking to a budget takes a lot of practical steps – you learned the best ones, expanding your knowledge on managing money.

- You took a step back to collect yourself – learning what financial goals are, how to set them, and how to make them as realistic as possible so that you can achieve them.

Now, you know how to approach money to create and manage a budget. Before this chapter is over, remember this – it takes a lot to learn, and it takes a lot to practice, too, but nothing is far from your grasp! Hone your budgeting skills with time, and until that time passes, let's move on to the next chapter and talk about a topic called debt!

CHAPTER 4

GOOD AND BAD DEBT

"A man who does not plan long ahead will find trouble right at his door."

Confucius.

Even in ancient times, having a good financial plan was necessary. It seemed like everything revolved around making good decisions, especially when you needed to take a risk and do something for yourself. The thing is, sometimes that risk pays off, and sometimes it doesn't. As a result of these choices, you will enter into what we know today as good and bad debt.

Most people (specifically young adults) view debt as a bad term, but it is not necessarily one. Only a handful know how to handle themselves whenever they come face to face with debt. This chapter puts you in the middle of that handful – because you will learn everything there is to know about this term.

Defining good and bad debt

A debate over good and bad debt has been ongoing for ages. People have discussed it in person, online, anywhere they can. But not all seemed to have found a definite explanation for debts and why they differ. Also, people don't even use the terms correctly, making the matter all the more confusing.

The reality is that there is a distinct line between good and bad debt, and it is all about what it does for you in the long run. Since you are a young adult, it is time for you to enter what is considered the core of the finance world and learn all about good and bad debt. Learn how to define and differentiate them and how they impact your budget.

The defining line between good and bad debt is the list of consequences. Here's the difference you need to know:

- Good debt is something you can benefit from in your life overall. Even if you are in debt right now, the benefits will remain there once you pay it off.

- Bad debt is the exact opposite – this type of debt does not give you any long-term benefits whatsoever. In this case, all you're left with is debt.

After reading this, you might think that good and bad debt are two very distinct and clear situations. This is where the line gets all blurry. It can be confusing to differentiate the two.

The thing you need to consider here before you begin managing your debt is the difference between good and bad debt. Let's dive a little more into this concept before we proceed.

Take buying an appliance as an example. If you invest in a technology appliance, then you get to reap the benefits from it long after you've paid off your debt. But in this case, as soon as you purchase your appliance, its value decreases, so it's a thin line you're walking. The same applies when you're buying a car. The moment you buy the vehicle, its value starts to decrease, so it will not give you plenty of value in the long run.

This, however, is not the case with property. Buying a house or an apartment fluctuates in value, meaning a mortgage can be a good debt. The value of the property you've invested in may decrease or increase in the future.

Sounds a bit confusing. Let's get into the details.

Some examples of GOOD debt are the following:

Mortgage – for most, this one is probably the best debt you will ever encounter. Property always had and always will have value, and this is something that generally increases over time.

Student loans – these are mostly considered good debts. Getting your education and earning a degree increases your value as an individual in the future. It can be something you build upon and will give you great advancement in the job market. This means more opportunities and bigger chances of increasing your net worth. That's why student loans are considered a good debt.

Investments – the exception to this rule is if you invest in anything that might potentially increase in value in the future. This applies to, for example, businesses, ventures and collector items. However, even in these cases, there are certain risks, and you might get stuck in bad debt. You need to be extremely careful here.

Some examples of BAD debt are the following:

Personal loans – any type of personal, short-term loan used by people in case of an emergency – and they never give you something back. Their interest rates are extremely high, and getting a personal loan may mean paying back with an interest rate as high as 300%.

Credit card debt – no matter what you buy with your card, it is mostly considered a bad loan. This is because credit cards have the highest interest rates, and depending on the item you purchase, these rates can either double or triple.

Most auto loans – I have already explained what most car loans are – a bad debt. The value you get of the car in the end doesn't really match what you've paid in the first place.

Pawn shop loans – exchanging an item of value for cash is only familiar to those who have been strapped for cash at some point in their life. This is when the value may decrease, but as soon as you go back for it, its value may just increase to a point where you can't afford it anymore. It is the definition of a bad debt.

Let's explain this concept a little further. The good and bad debt are, of course, both debts, only with the former, while you get into debt, you have a certain way of getting out of it. With the bad debt - you're just in debt.

The defining line can become even more complex - let's say for example that you want to purchase a car. When you want to make this kind of a purchase (a larger one) you basically have two options - either you buy it with cash, or you buy it with financing. This is where things get interesting. When you buy your car with cash, all of your money will be tied to that particular purchase. But on the other hand, should you decide to buy it with financing, you only need so much to cover the down payment. So, you would take the financing and buy the car you want, but with the rest of your cash, you can invest the remaining amount, and even get a higher interest in that than the interest of your loan. By doing this, with the returns of the investments, you can get some help in paying back your initial loan. This is a good debt. In simpler terms - one you have a solid plan to get out of before you even take it.

Managing student loans and other common debts

You are a young adult, and this is probably something that would interest you the most right now. Taking care of your student debt (or some other common debts) is part of getting your finances in order. If you are just starting college or finishing college, or you have a debt you want to get rid of, it is understandable to want to know how to approach this accurately. Even if you plan to take out a student loan, the right strategies are key.

On the other hand, "putting all your eggs in one basket" as they say, is the bad kind of debt - one you should avoid as much as possible. The thing is, life happens, and sometimes, due to the challenges you are faced with, you may come face to face with bad debts, and in these situations, you should have detailed steps on how to get out of it. The following segment includes getting out of debt overall - a layout of tips that can help you rise above all the curveballs of life.

Managing student loans can be either tricky or easy business – depending on your point of view and the action steps you take. If you want to pay them off as soon as possible, here are some tips you can implement!

Make a plan.

Creating a plan that outlines exactly how you will manage your income and expenses is a great first step. If you have a student loan you need to repay, you should make a solid plan and track how much of your income can be allocated to the repayment every month. This will not only help you set aside a solid amount each month, but it will also prevent you from overspending elsewhere.

Instead of guessing or thinking of an approximate number, look into how many loans you have - that will give you the total amount of what you should repay.

Refinance and automate.

When you refinance your student loan, you consolidate the existing loans into one loan to get a lower interest rate. In the long run, this can help you reduce your interest rate significantly – and because of that, it has become an appealing option to many. Interest rates have been dropping over the years, and if you have a good credit score and no negative marks, then you have the golden chance to use this tip and demonstrate smart financial behaviour.

Knowing the loan terms can also help you budget accordingly, this can help you dedicate just the right amount from your income every month, and with a lower interest rate. From that point on, to make things a lot easier for you, you can automate your payments to make sure you pay on time, all the time.

Go through the most popular assistance programs.

The first section is the government - always there to help you out, especially in the case of federal student loans. With their help, you can manage your debt by enrolling in an assistance program. By being a borrower, you can check if you are eligible for these government programs before you make your decision. Many deferment and forbearance options can provide you with reduced monthly payments based on your income. Keep in mind that these only apply to federal student loans.

The second section is your employer – some companies offer assistance programs that are specifically created to help employees pay off student loans. The contributions they make and the help they offer vary from one company to another. For example, they can help you make payments on your loan, give you the option of access to refinancing, and even offer to fully repay the loan after you've worked there a certain amount of time (and showcased your skills). Whatever option they give out, it is usually something you can communicate with them – that's what makes these companies an attractive option for many young adults.

Start budgeting properly.

As a borrower*, there are many practical ways to implement proper budgeting if you want to manage your loans successfully. The most common approach people take is saving money. This is a practical solution, and it has helped reduce both student and other types of loans. It is the basis of doing proper budgeting with the money available to you. Each month, you can dedicate a certain amount to minimizing your loans or debts by focusing on saving money. Try doing one of the many things – using public transportation instead of a car while traveling to work, searching for discounts when purchasing something, and taking advantage of free or discounted resources available on your campus (when you are a student). With a lot of careful planning and taking advantage of all resources at hand, you can stay on top of your student loan payments.

**Borrower is someone who received a certain amount of money with the obligation to pay it back (most of the time with interest).*

Remember, getting rid of your student loan is not unmanageable – all you need is a proactive and highly organized approach – and that's exactly what you will get here.

Strategies for debt repayment and avoiding excessive debt

As you grow, the student loan might not be the only debt you have. No person wants to have a debt, but these things may happen, most of the time, without you even noticing them. Some people believe that going into debt is completely out of their control, but nothing can be farther from the truth.

Even if you happen to go into bad debt, there is always a way out. Correct – it will take a lot of prioritizing, but the strategies you will learn here are ones you will follow for the rest of your life. It is in situations such as these that you will learn how to strategize and do everything in your power to achieve your goal - getting out of debt.

Avoiding excessive debt and the best strategies for debt repayment are as follows:

1. One of the most dangerous things that are closer than you think is credit cards. I mentioned them earlier in this chapter as a part of the bad debt, and I meant it. They create the illusion of being able to pay for something when, in reality,

you can't. If there is one good rule you can live by, it is this one – if you cannot afford it without a credit card, then you should probably refrain from buying it.

So, what's your strategy here? Open your wallet and check how many credit cards you have. Check your balance on each of them and write it down. See how many of these make you drag along debt and focus on them. Go down into specifics - how you will repay it, when, etc.

2. If you do have a credit card, try to limit its use and limit the amount of credit cards you have. The more credit cards you have, the more interest and payments you have to make. Doing this will minimize your chances of effectively and responsibly handling your cards. Instead of losing track of your expenses, have one card and keep track of everything.

    So, what's your strategy here? Once you've repaid the critical cards, go down to one or two cards that you will use. Add a limit to them, and only use them in cases of emergencies.

3. Build up that emergency fund we talked about before. Having a safety net is important; someone should tell you this and nudge you toward saving rather than having to experience it firsthand. Life throws you curveballs all the time. Literally, anything could happen – you could lose your job, you could sustain an injury that would prevent you from doing your job for a while, or anything unexpected may happen. This is when you should rely on the money you've saved rather than going into debt.

    So, what's your strategy here? Paying off your debt was the first step, but the second is trying not to get into new debt by simply allocating your finances elsewhere - to your savings account. It is one of the smartest moves you'll ever make, creating that safety net I mentioned, instead of running into a bad situation once again.

4. Focus on what you need rather than what you want. Let's face it: every single one of us has needs and wants. But in this case, what separates you from a financially responsible adult is focusing on your wants rather than your needs. By tweaking and changing your perspective (and your spending habits), you can improve your finances and manage debt.

    So, what's your strategy here? The emergency fund is exactly what I'm talking about in this case. Being a responsible adult means looking into the future. Another way you can practice this strategy is by investing your money - but more on that later on.

5. Budgeting may be difficult, but it is necessary. It is a way of tracking where your money goes in a month. You will also be able to see how much you have saved, how much you have spent (and where), and prioritize your debt, too. Think of tracking your finances as tracking your success – after a few months of doing good budgeting, you will immediately notice a difference.

    So, what's your strategy here? As you can see, every strategy goes on top of one another - you start with paying off your debt, checking your cards, making a plan on how to repay it, saving for rainy days, investing, and now living on a budget. To some of you this may sound like a scary concept, but what's scarier - living on a budget or living with a debt? Calculate how much you need for the basic monthly expenses - you know what to do with the rest.

6. As luck would have it, you may get a pay increase. What to do with this unexpected cash influx? The answer to this question is simple – either put that money aside for rainy days or use it toward your debt management – either way, they are more than welcome!

So, what's your strategy here? This is the easiest (and the least probable) thing to happen to you, but if you're lucky enough, you might get that extra money - just enough to cover your monthly payments. This, along with all the other strategies I mentioned just now, can help you get rid of excessive debt and help you stay as far away from debt as possible.

What did you learn from this chapter?

- There is a difference between bad debt and good debt.
- Knowing what good and bad debt are will help you make better financial choices.
- Look into the options that can help you manage student and other common loans.
- Some incredible strategies to avoid and manage debt – lifelong knowledge on making the most out of your finances and current situation.

Navigating the financial terrain can be a challenge for many, especially when you are a young adult. But that should not stop you from going after what you want! Doing that will soon lead you to the next door you need to open and think about - credit cards and credit scores. With this in mind, we are turning the page together and walking straight into a room filled with useful information. It is time to start learning that everything you do counts.

CHAPTER 5

A NEW TERRAIN - CREDIT CARDS AND CREDIT SCORES

"Plastic is the money of our generation."

Anthony T. Hincks

I t seems that, in the world of finances, every number counts. With that in mind, you need to know how to deal with what the world knows as a credit card and a credit score. In this chapter, you will learn that these two are very important parts of your journey to financial independence. Your future depends on the relationship you build with them, so read this chapter carefully.

How to use credit cards responsibly

It is of utmost importance to know how to use credit cards. Learning this can help you maintain your financial stability and can help you avoid debt overall. The thing is, not many people focus on the severity of the consequences of having a credit card, and they only focus on the perks. Don't get me wrong, there are many perks, but when you're young, and not financially literate, you have a higher chance of using the credit card in a way that will make you accumulate debt. Managing credit cards responsibly will be one of the main topics of this chapter. To understand how to do that you need a detailed guide - and I have made sure you have just the thing you need!

Understanding the concept of credit cards

Before going deep into the guide, you need to understand how credit cards work. In a way, it is sort of a way of borrowing money. Using that payment method constantly means you are constantly borrowing money from the issuer, while constantly agreeing to pay that amount back to them at a later stage.

1.   **Start with your financial status quo**

To get a credit card you need to apply for one first. Before doing that, take a look at your current financial state. Take your expenses and your income into consideration and see if you have the means to repay the debts from the credit card you're about to make. By doing this, you will know whether you are financially stable enough to get a credit card. Also, from all the options you may come across, choose the one that will fit your needs and finances the most.

2.   **Choosing the credit card**

Let's talk a little bit about that now, shall we? There is a plateau of different credit cards available, all of them ready to fit anyone's needs and lifestyle. Some of them offer small rewards such as cashback. Others offer incredibly low interest rates and travel perks. From all the options that may be in front of you, choose the one that has the most straightforward terms and conditions, the best annual fees, and the best interest rates.

3. Start budgeting

To successfully manage your finances, you need to set your budget - and know it on a monthly basis, including everything you put on your credit card. As you can notice, it all comes down to tracking your income and expenses at the same time so you can understand how much money you spend, and where. Take your necessities, your bills, and your savings into account. Include the credit card payments in your budget too. Making a budget means you should be able to cover all your expenses without going over it.

4. Paying your balance

Each month, you need to be able to pay your balance in full. This is one of the most important rules if you want to use your credit card responsibly. Avoiding interest rates is a must. Avoiding excessive debt is a must too. By paying your balance in full every month you maintain a good credit score. Set up the automatic payment we talked about in the earlier chapters and that way, you will never miss a deadline.

5. Check how much you spend

We all want something that is a little bit out of our grasp at the moment. This can be anything from fancier clothes to a luxury vacation. But, and this is important, you need to monitor how much you spend each month. Keeping track of your spending means that you will know how much you need to get through the month, bills and everything, leaving you just enough room to "wiggle" around. Note your spending patterns, identify any possible issue, and make adjustments to your spending as you go.

6. Refrain from spending too much on impulse

Having a credit card in your pocket seems like you have something you can just "swipe" any time you want something. The credit card looks like it can make all your dreams come true. However, lack of physical cash in your pocket can make you go into debt very easily. No matter how difficult it is, try to refrain from spending a lot of money.

7. Have a low credit utilization

The credit utilization means the percentage of available credit you're using at the moment. By keeping it low, preferably below 30%, you can maintain a good credit score. If it is high, then you have probably maxed out your credit cards, and you have stretched yourself too thin (financially).

8. Always check the fees

Fees are always there, embedded into the fine print of your credit card agreement. They vary and they can be late payment fees, balance transfer fees, annual fees, etc. As soon as you familiarize yourself with how your credit card works, you will be able to avoid any of those fees.

9. Use the rewards

And use them wisely! Every credit card nowadays comes with some kind of a reward - be it points, miles, cashback, or something else. I suggest you take full advantage of the reward payment programs, and benefit from your spending. But the line here is incredibly thin - try not to overspend just so you can earn a specific reward.

10. Check your statements

A part of being financially responsible is checking your payments regularly. Verify all the transactions you have made on a monthly basis and check if there are any unauthorized charges. This way, you can easily spot any fraudulent behavior and protect your credit score.

11. Credit history

This is something that you build over time, as a responsible credit card user. Such behavior may serve you in the future if you plan to apply for a loan or a mortgage. It is all about managing your credit in a responsible way - such as paying your bills on time, keeping your credit utilization low, etc.

12. Prepare for the worst-case scenario

All of us want to avoid this, but in case it happens, you should come prepared. Think about having a credit card with an available credit line. This can give you a safety net in case any unexpected expenses happen. But, in this case, keep in mind you should pay these off as soon as possible, as they come with a sky-high interest.

Understanding Credit Score

To further learn how to navigate through the field of finances, you need to know something about credit scores. For this particular topic, let's start from the very beginning.

The credit score consists of three digits that show whether you are an okay candidate for a credit to any creditors and lenders. The information that is gathered to create this number comes from your credit report. This number shows the lender everything they need to assess the risk of giving you money.

But how is the credit score actually created?

There are a few segments that play a particularly important role here. Here are the components of a credit score:

1. Your payment history - is about 35% of your overall credit score. By far the most valuable contributor to your credit score - it reflects whether you have submitted all your bills on time, and whether you have had any late payments.

2. Your credit utilization - is about 30% of your overall credit score. This represents the credit you are using at the moment compared to your total available credit. This is what I mentioned earlier - if you keep it below 30%, you have a good credit score.

3. Your credit history - is about 15% of your overall credit score. It shows the duration of time that you've been using credit. Generally, the older credit history is something that the lenders prefer.

4. Your type of credit - is about 10% of your credit score. When the lenders are viewing your information, they would prefer to see a mix of credit types, such as mortgages, installment loans, credit cards, etc. The variety in your credit portfolio can positively impact your overall credit score.

5. Your new credit - is about 10% of your credit score. For example, if you open a few new credit accounts in a short period of time, the lenders will assume you are in financial distress. This may lower your credit score.

After knowing what credit score is and what it consists of, it is time to turn to its importance. Below you will find a few reasons why credit scores are so important.

- Access to credit - a good credit score will open up a lot of doors for you - meaning new opportunities, including mortgages, credit cards, and loans. The lenders will assess the risk of lending you money.

- Interest rate - the credit score will affect the interest rate you receive on your credit cards and your loans. The higher credit score mostly means lower interest rates - which will save you some money over time.

- Premium insurance - the insurance companies nowadays use credit scores to determine the insurance for rent, home, and auto. The higher credit score may mean lower insurance premium, as it means lower risk.

- Rental applications - the property management companies as well as the landlords check the credit scores as a part of the application process. A good credit score may increase the chance of you being approved for rental housing.

- Job opportunities - even though this is not that common, some employers may review the credit score as a part of the job hiring process, especially for positions that require financial literacy. A good credit score may just get you the job you want!

- Services and utilities - the service providers and utility companies may check the credit score if you want to set up a new account with them. A good credit score may help you get lower deposit fees.

After this, you may ask yourself how can you get a good credit score, and maintain it? The first thing you need to do is pay your bills on time. By doing this, you maintain a good credit score. I cannot emphasize the importance of automatic payments here. Make sure to set that up and you won't have any worries.

Then, you may just want to try not to max out your credit cards. Constantly monitor your credit report and check for any errors or erratic behavior on your part. Avoid opening a lot of new credit accounts within a short period of time and try to have a mix of credit types to improve your overall score.

Tips for building and maintaining a good credit score

With credit score, as we move further deep into the chapter, you will notice that everything comes down to financial stability. No matter what your goal is - improving your score or establishing credit, here are a few tips that can help you achieve that. You are already familiar with some of them, while the others are brand new, but there's one thing they all have in common - they're incredibly helpful and will set you on the right path of financial independence!

- Always pay your bills on time. No matter what happens, try to be as consistent as you possibly can with your payments. The payment history you have is the most important thing about your credit score. So, making sure that all your bills are settled will help you avoid any negative impacts on your overall credit score.

- Keep the credit utilization low. Keeping the credit card balance to your credit limits means you are doing a good job. A high utilization ratio may have a negative impact on your overall credit score. To keep a healthy score, try to stay below 30%.

- Diversity is key. A diverse credit mix means a positive impact on your credit score. In this case, while you are maintaining that diversity, try not to overdo it. By that, I mean there is no need to open new credit accounts within a short period, especially if you can manage those you already have perfectly well.

- Try not to close old accounts. Why? Credit history is important, and it just may be the determining factor of your credit score. If you close the old credit accounts you will automatically shorten your credit history, thus lowering your overall score. Keep the accounts active and open, even if you don't use them frequently.

- Monitor your reports. Create a schedule where you review your credit report and make that as frequently as on a monthly basis. Check for any irregularities or errors, and should that happen, act accordingly. Your reports should always reflect accurate information.

- Limit your new credit inquiries. Every time you apply for new credit, there is a hard inquiry which is recorded on your credit report. In the future, this may lower your credit score. Limit the number of new credit inquiries, and try to apply for credit only when necessary. Also, when you apply for credit, try to be as selective as possible about the offers in front of you.

- Automatize your payments. Consider these the ultimate words of wisdom. If you miss a payment on any type of bill, then it may have a great impact on your credit score. By setting automatic payments, you will never have to worry about a payment deadline. This will help you avoid late fees and keep a straight payment record.

- The credit should be used responsibly. A responsible use of the credit you get means you will maintain a good credit score. Stay committed and borrow only as much as you can repay. You don't need a high balance on your credit card. The credit should only be used to help you wisely manage the finances instead of overspending.

- Consistency is important. Patience is important too. Creating and maintaining a good credit score takes time, effort, and patience. It takes consistent financial habits. To achieve your goal, you need to stay committed, and as time passes, you will be able to both achieve and maintain this.

- The help of a professional is always a good idea. If you feel like you cannot make it on your own here, but still want to do everything to improve your credit score, then you can always seek assistance from a financial advisor. They have the knowledge and experience to provide you with the guidance you need as well as the additional strategies to achieve the credit score you want.

How to obtain and review your credit report for accuracy

Now, we move on to the next step, which is reviewing your credit report for accuracy. Being "in good financial health" means knowing that all the information shown on your credit report is correct. The best way to help you get to the bottom of this is to follow a step-by-step guide, as shown below.

1. Start by requesting your credit report. You are entitled to one free credit report every 12 months. There is an authorized website called Annual Credit Report, where you can get it for free as mandated by federal law.

2. Select the reports. Once you are on the site, follow the instructions to fill in the request.

3. Verify your identity. In order to access your credit reports, you will need some personal information to confirm your identity. This usually includes anything from a social security number to a date of birth and current address. There may even be some security questions.

4. It is time to check your credit scores. To make sure you're thorough and have checked all the necessary information, pay close attention to the four main sectors - personal info, account info, inquiries, and public records. You already know what should be included in the personal info (your name, address, and other personal details), as well as the account info (your list of accounts, loans, credit cards, etc). In the section inquiries, check whether you have had any in the past period, and verify that the ones you have are from you. Finally, within the section public records, look for anything that may appear on your credit report - tax liens, foreclosures, and so on. Make sure everything is up to date.

5. Take action if you notice any discrepancies. You have the right to do that - process your dispute online, by phone, or via email. To support your statement, add the relevant documentation. Do a follow-up to ensure it is resolved.

6. Do this monitoring regularly. Make a habit out of it. Reviewing your credits at least once a year will help you maintain your credit score and take full control over your financial situation. You can even subscribe to some credit monitoring services that provide alerts any time the credit report changes.

These simple rules will do so much more for you than you imagine. As a young adult, someone who is just stepping into the shoes of a financially responsible person, you need to remember that it is all about having the correct and latest information. If that isn't the case, now you know how to act on it (and fast) and ultimately protect your financial stability.

Now let's talk a little bit about those plastic things we know as credit cards.

Borrowing money through credit cards has something called APR (Annual Percentage Rate). It plays a crucial role in borrowing money. To make a fully informed financial decision, you need to know how credit cards function too. Let's take a look at it together.

Types of credit card interest rates

As I just mentioned the APRs, here is what you need to know about the different types.

- Purchase APR - this is applied to any purchase you make with the credit card. You can even carry the balance from one month to the next, by not paying the statement balance in full, and get an interest charge on the purchase APR.

- Balance transfer APR - depending on the credit card you choose, you may receive a promotional balance transfer APR, which will allow you to transfer a balance from other credit cards at a decreased rate. But this usually only happens for a promotional period.

- Cash advance APR - any cash advances that involve withdrawing cash from an ATM usually have a higher interest rate than the purchases. The cash advance APR applies to these transactions.

Factors that affect credit card interest rates

Believe it or not, the interest rates vary due to several factors. When it comes to credit cards, these are the ones you should know:

- Your credit score - here is how the credit score and credit cards are connected. The one significantly influences the other. The ones that have higher credit scores usually have lower interest rates, and vice versa - all depending on the perceived risk.

- The market conditions - the credit card interest rates also change as the market current changes too. There are broad economic factors that play a crucial role in this, including market competition, and inflation.

- Type of credit card - this too plays a big role. Depending on the card you have, the interest rates, benefits, and features will vary.

- The limit of the credit card - last but not least, we have the spending limit. It represents the maximum amount of credit extended to the cardholder (you).

This last line might have confused you for a moment there, so this is why I am expounding on it too. Understanding the credit card limits can help you manage your spending better and maximize the efficiency of the credit card itself.

The initial credit limit is important. This is set up based on a few factors, such as your income, your existing debt (should you have any) and how worthy you are to receive credit. As time passes, this limit may be adjusted.

Then, you need to consider the credit utilization ratio. This is where your credit card balance is compared to your credit limit. Keeping the credit balance low can positively impact your credit score. Remember, the ratio should be below 30% for a healthy credit score.

To go back a few lines, the credit limit may increase. If your issuer notices that you have responsibly used your credit card, they may increase the limit. As much as this leads to bigger flexibility, it is also a bigger responsibility too - you still need to manage this correctly and avoid overspending.

Finally, the security of the credit card itself. As the chapter slowly comes to its end, we are going to see all the credit card security measures that are usually set in place. These are essential for preventing any unauthorized use of the credit card. As a credit card holder, you need to know its protection features - here they are:

- Monitoring for fraud - nowadays, there are sophisticated fraud detection systems that can monitor your activity and notice any fraudulent behavior. These systems are mostly flagging unusual behavior or transactions that are inconsistent with the regular behavior or transaction of the owner of the card (you).

- Zero liability protection - according to the federal law, the cardholders are usually not held liable for any unauthorized transactions made with their credit cards. Should this happen to you, you deem yourself protected simply by reporting it.

- EMV chip technology - EMV stands for Europay, Matercard, and Visa. Their chip technology has raised the bar on security features compared to the regular magnetic stripe cards. These chips hold a unique transaction code for each individual purchase. That makes it more difficult for any fraud to clone the card.

- Protected purchasing - all cards offer purchase protection benefits. These may vary - from price protection and coverage against theft or damaged items which are purchased with the card - it is all about understanding the limitations and terms so you can maximize their use.

However, even with these security measures in place, I would still advise you to monitor your credit card transactions and activities. The monthly statement, the account activity, and transaction alerts can help you react fast in case of an uncomfortable situation.

What did you learn from this chapter?

- The amazing power of credit cards

- What a credit score is and how to maintain a good one

- A part of delivering an accurate financial representation to yourself is frequently checking your credit reports.

- Interest rates - how they happen and how they affect you.

To conclude this chapter, the interest rates, the limits, the credit cards, and the credit scores are imperative for a responsible use of that little piece of plastic. To make an informed decision about it, you need to be familiarized with it first - which just happened!

However, after taking this chapter into account, it seems like one crucial topic has escaped us. After all, we talked about how to manage money, how to spend it wisely, and even how to save it and steer clear from financial trouble. But there's one thing we have yet to discover - how to make money. After all, you can't spend money if you don't have it in the first place, right? Turn the page to discover your best choices for becoming financially independent.

64

CHAPTER 6

HOW TO MAKE MONEY

*"Money isn't everything, but it's right up
there with oxygen."*

Zig Ziglar

As much as you hate to admit it, this is true – creating a comfortable lifestyle for yourself is not really an option if you don't have a steady and strong income. But, for some young adults, this is easier said than done. Even though we live in the era of technology, where everything is there, at the tips of your fingers, when it comes down to the actual part of making money, some of you may feel stuck. And I understand that. I was once where you are now – stranded in a sea of possibilities, yet still feeling like none of them suited me.

That changed when I started learning about how to make money. In the end, it turned out that it was an approach based on multiple viewpoints, one of them being the key point – determination. Instead of ignoring money and thinking that nothing will ever work for you, start focusing on prioritizing money and seeing how everything around you will start changing.

Let's delve into the chapter and learn all about how to make money and afford the lifestyle you want.

Cast a wide net - learn about all the ways you can generate income

The world of today is dynamic – it is filled with opportunities but also with an ever-changing job market. That leads to certain economic instabilities. The academic achievement you have made is excellent. Still, the process of obtaining a degree leaves you with a significant gap where you might have focused on honing the skills for the practical aspect of life, including generating income and financial literacy.

That is the reason why, when most students leave college, they are baffled with their choices and don't know where to proceed. They don't clearly understand how to leverage their skills and gain financial independence. This is the reason why it's important to focus on learning about finances, too. It is about you getting the wind beneath your wings to develop a unique and innovative approach that will expand your income-generating opportunities. That kind of mindset is what promotes growth and resilience whenever you are faced with a challenge.

First things first- take a look at the opportunities you have. As a young adult, you have more opportunities than you can imagine. However, most young adults walk the path that is the most familiar - which is also known as the broader concept of making money.

While you concentrate on finding the right job opportunity for you, you go through some of the most common (and popular) job options. These are all a good choice, and since you are at an early stage of your entrance into the workforce, you are in a very unique position. Here are the most common choices you can make in terms of choosing your income source.

- Getting a regular job - most young adults see getting a regular job as the perfect opportunity to reach financial independence. When it comes to picking a job, it can either be something you've learned to do your whole life or shifting your focus to monetizing a hobby of yours.

- Trying out freelancing - From an early age, you get to concentrate on finding various money vessels and even completely dismiss the concept of working the regular 9-5 job. Freelancing is the way to do that. With it, you have the unique opportunity to explore the various ways you can complete a job, without having to work the regular 40 hours a week. Freelancing can also help you cast an even wider net as you try communicating with people from all over the world and collaborate with them on various kinds of projects.

- Entrepreneurship - giving this one a go takes a lot of guts, but it might turn out to be one of the best ones for you. If you have a plan or an idea for a business (something that you can actively work on, at least in the beginning), entrepreneurship may be the right call for you. Acting on this idea may create the market disruption you need. It may also give you the opportunity to become visible to potential clients and competitors, thus developing a long-term vision for your financial life.

As you can notice, this book doesn't really delve deep into the regular jobs. The reason for that is because the regular job is just that - regular, something we are all familiar with. As a young adult, you most likely know how to get that kind of job already. I am here to help you cast a wider net, open your mind to new possibilities, and thrive. Now, let's move on to the main aspects you need to focus on to make the most out of your working journey.

Think about your skills - your skills are what separates you from the crowd. Define what you know and what you can offer as a product or a service, and then start from there. This is the most important aspect because it sets the groundwork for everything else you're going to do later on. Keep in mind, these can be more than one skill or passions. On most occasions, people mix a few of their passions to create something unique later on.

Choose your niche - as you can notice, these three aspects go hand in hand, as you can't move on from one to another. As you do these three in sync, you will realize that this third one is just as important. Choosing your niche means identifying exactly what you want to do based on your passions and skills. You have a particular expertise in a certain field, and don't be afraid to promote that.

Network - to spread the word about what you offer, to create a good web of people to work with, to dive deep into the freelance and entrepreneurship market, first you need to network. Do that by going to events where you can meet a lot of people who are more experienced in your field of choice. Talk to them, get their opinion, their experience, and avoid the mistakes they've been making.

Determining how you can make a grander effect in terms of freelancing and entrepreneurship takes a lot more than simply discovering what you know and love. After determining that, you can move on to the following:

1. Combine your skills and interests and come up with one or two things you can do, sell, or market online that would result in some income. This can be anything that you put your mind to – from graphic design to writing or maybe even teaching.

2. Explore the online platforms. This will help you choose the right platform where you can make the most out of your skillset and reach your desired audience. You can try platforms like YouTube, TikTok, or Etsy, depending on what you want to do.

3. Start working on developing your content. At the end of your brainstorming, there must be some product or service that you will be determined to offer. Create some content where you show your abilities, and make sure it is focused on the target group you want to attract. You can make blog posts, short videos, podcasts – anything you like.

4. Start building up your online presence. What does this mean? It means that if you want to generate a strong income, you need to focus on using social media channels to promote your content. Make your audience as engaged as possible and build your credibility one step at a time.

5. Finally, start to turn profits. The last step is selling your product or service, including ads in your blog, doing some affiliate marketing, offering some sponsored content, and reviewing products, etc.

This is the simple framework that can be used to build and promote almost any kind of venture you come up with.

Stepping away from the traditional 9-5 job and generating your income elsewhere takes time, determination, and thinking outside the box. However, this is still an option worth exploring because when you start, you seem to be given a blank canvas. You can do anything you want with it.

Delving deeper – side hustles

As a young mind that manages to shape their own future, so far you are doing great! You're stepping away from the familiarity that comes with having a regular job and you are creating something completely yours - from scratch. As you've established that, after some time, you might seem like you can take on some more work. Or you might even think that you still have other skills to show off, and to do this, you need to look into other job opportunities.

In the previous section, we only touched upon the subject of turning your interests into money-makers. The power of entrepreneurship and freelancing is great, and you can utilize it to the extent you need - as long as you determine the aspect you just read.

In this section, we will talk more about it – the power of the side hustle. It includes everything we mentioned earlier – from identifying your skills to monetizing them. You have probably noticed some of the more popular side-hustle options - product reviews, affiliate marketing, etc. The reason why the market has been seeing a lot of them lately is because of their high success rate – offering the perfect side hustle. If you decide to take this seriously, you will manage to sustain the lifestyle you want and never compromise on its quality.

First things first - what are side hustles? These are additional sources of income that people pursue along with their primary job. These are an excellent way to hone your skills, to try something new and exciting, and to create some new skills on top of the ones you've already acquired. But the thing is, even though many people are familiar with this concept, not many people turn to it - mostly because they don't know where to begin. Luckily for you, you have this book in your hands, so that shouldn't be an issue for you.

It's all about getting started easily. If you are still on the fence about it, here are a few things why you should do it, and a few tips to get you started.

- Yes, the additional income is always welcome, but there is also a potential opportunity for growth. By exploring various ideas, you also explore various potential ways of making money. It is the creative process that will spark up your imagination in unknown and wonderful directions.

- Tracking your finances while having extra security. For many people, developing a side hustle is both an enjoyment and a security blanket. You get to see how your ideas grow, and at the same time, the amount on your bank statement grows as well.

- Go after what you love. For some, it is more than just the money (though it is always a good addition). Sometimes, people get to explore themselves and discover a whole new range of things they want to do. Those things may not turn out to be full-time job material, so the side hustle is an excellent solution.

- It is a flexible endeavor. Stepping away into a non-traditional job terrain is the perfect choice for some people. Having a side hustle often comes with a flexible schedule and may allow you to do everything you want in a day.

- Creating an entrepreneurship future. As a concept, it allows you to bounce off of ideas without risking a lot. It can be the base upon which you may build a customer net and the chance to gain opportunities and even look to the future possibilities of launching your own business or businesses.

Generally, the side hustle can provide you with many benefits and open so many doors for you that you might end up creating a start-up from something you previously called a hobby. You get to enjoy some financial security, as this can be a way for you to develop a reasonable emergency fund or close off any debts you have. On top of everything, think about your own personal fulfillment! It is an unmatched feeling to know that you have started something from scratch and that you are working on it with every fiber of your being! It is a chance for both personal and professional development. You may not know exactly where you'll end up, but I promise you, if you are determined, it will be a good place.

Balancing multiple income streams and your personal life

It seems like there is a lot of talk about how to create the most out of your mind and hobbies and to use your free time to generate income. As a young adult, this might be more interesting to you than you can imagine. The thrill of finding out how you can create a solid income stream out of something you truly love is fascinating – and things get even better if you have more hobbies you can profit from. But when do you stop to say, "enough is enough"? Sometimes, and this happens especially among young people, plunging into the workforce and creating these new side hustles takes up so much of your time that you hardly ever have the time to turn around and check on yourself and your personal life.

When this happens, you may not realize it initially, but after a while, you may find yourself in the middle of a vortex you have difficulty getting out of. During your journey of creating a good professional future for yourself, it is important not to forget your personal life, too. Managing good relationships with yourself, your family, and your friends is the fuel that keeps you going in life, at least most of the time.

Creating solid streams of income, especially high income, requires constant and active involvement. Running a business is difficult and having a few of these sources to juggle may be a little too much to handle. In most professional experiences, managing a few side hustles at the same time can leave almost no time for maintaining a private life. That's when good organization comes into the picture.

There are three effective ways you can manage your multiple income streams and your private life – here they are.

1. Keep yourself organized

And I don't mean only a few days in the week – I mean all the time! Having an organized time means you can dedicate an exact amount of it to yourself, to work as you have planned, and to dedicate enough time to your family. Here, you can incorporate a few principles to make that happen, among which – you can start by setting realistic work goals. This is the easy bit, as many successful people do this. Your goals may be challenging, but they all need to be realistic. When you look at your tasks for the day, if you feel like someone else can do a better job at a few of those tasks, or you don't have the time to do all of them, it is more than okay to outsource them to other people, such as freelancers (as long as they are the right choice). That will help you maintain a better time management technique and work-life balance. Don't be scared of losing some of your profits.

Freeing up your time is always a worthy investment, and most likely, the person you'll be working with will complete the tasks better than you would.

You should also know when you are working vs when you're not. No matter how much you try, you always seem to take the work home with you. You are working even when you're not supposed to – during dinner, during your quality time with yourself, and with the people you love. Having a workspace can help a lot, especially if you decide to run a few side hustles. You need to remember – when the time for work is over, it is really over.

That leads me to the next principle: having a separate space where you conduct your work. You can't work and relax from your own bed – you need to have a dedicated nook in the home (if you prefer working from home) and finish all your work there. This can help you disconnect when you need some time to relax and unwind. Without implementing this separation, you may end up struggling to find the balance between your work and your private life.

2. Take a step beyond being productive

What does this mean? It means always choosing efficiency over productivity. As you focus on setting up some incredible income streams for yourself, you may find yourself constantly making checklists and checking things off all the time. Doing this for a longer period may result in severe burnout. Instead of that, turn to a smarter approach – look at your goals rather than your journey, and brainstorm for some more efficient ways to achieve what you set out to do.

3. Define your motivation

Find out the reason why – why have you set out to achieve certain professional goals? Why do you take so much of your time to dedicate to it? Why do you want to create a work-life balance? The answers to these questions will lead you to define your motivation. They will lead you to work at full speed ahead but with a steady and determined mind.

Without clearly defining your motivation, you might have difficulty dedicating your hours. You may be working hard to provide for yourself or to help out your family – no matter what the cause, you need to have it clearly defined. That will crystalize the image for you, making it easier to dedicate just the right amount of time to work and for social connections.

What did you learn from this chapter?

- How to focus on money and prioritizing yourself.

- The importance of exploring various income-generating opportunities.

- The power of freelancing and entrepreneurship, and how to get started.

- How to make the most out of the best digital platforms today.

- Getting to know the power of the side hustle and how it can change your life and your mindset.

- How to refrain from giving it all in one place – creating the perfect balance between your professional and private life.

Making money may be a challenge for some of you, but as you can see from this chapter, it is all about finding the thing you want to do. You are a young adult, and you have both the time and the resources to explore until you discover the true you. Once you do, all you need is to sit down, work and research a little bit, and set up the side hustle that may generate a lot of passive income. As soon as you know it, you might be looking into a decent amount in your bank account.

This is when the question may pose itself – what to do with all that money? Is there any way to expand your money-making ventures? If this question pops into your mind, then you're headed in the right direction! You're already thinking about the future, and I like that! In this book, the future is in the next chapter – because it is all about investing and multiplying the money you've made!

CHAPTER 7

HOW TO MULTIPLY YOUR MONEY – INVESTMENTS

*"Personal finance is only 20% head knowledge.
It's 80% behavior!"*

Dave Ramsey.

The uniqueness of approaching money comes from every individual's different perspective. But even in this case, we all have some things in common – starting from financial stability. Once you feel it, you want to make sure it lasts for as long as you live, right? So, you turn to various sources to figure out how to multiply your money and make it last as long as possible. In other words, you're investing in them.

This is a very positive money habit, right up there with creating a safety net and a budget. Investing is the peak reflection of your financial activities, and it is a combination of knowledge and behavior. Throughout this entire chapter you will be reading about investments - allow it to be the ultimate creative vessel through which your imagination will roam wild. While reading, you will learn about various ideas and ways you could get your money to grow.

That being the case, please don't take this as a definitive guide to investing. Why? Because this is a very deep and vast subject, and from this perspective, we are only talking about the tip of the iceberg here. To fully master investing you will need a lot more than this. If you want to apply yourself to this subject, you will need plenty of additional studying, and maybe even some assistance from a financial advisor.

While reading this chapter, you might discover you're already aligned with this on some points – that's your behavior. Learning about the rest – that's knowledge.

Let's dive in.

The basics of investing for beginners

Investing can be complex to understand, but it is the basis upon which personal finance is built. Learning this will help you keep track of the latest market movements and boost your confidence and your next financial moves.

The simplest way to explain this is to begin by understanding what you want and then just going for it. I reckon you need some more information at this time, so here is everything you need to do, explained in detail.

- You need to decide what your goals are – before you start looking into some investment options, you need to consider your overarching goals. Do you want to generate more income, or do you want to invest in something long-term? Once you decide on which option you want to take, it will narrow down your choices. This step of the process is about understanding your goals and the timeframe you need to achieve them. It will help you determine the risk you need to take and which aspect to prioritize. For example, if you want to invest in a retirement plan, then you need to take a look into your IRA and 401(k), whether your employer offers one, and how to get the most out of it.

- Choose your investment vehicles next – this can be one vehicle or more, depending on your goals. Think investing accounts. Think about developing a portfolio. Think brokerage accounts. With the help of the brokerage account, you can sell and buy stocks, ETFs, and mutual funds. This is a flexible way to invest, as there is no income limit or a limit on how much you can invest. There are also no rules if you want to withdraw your funds. The only drawback to it is that you do not have the same tax advantage as with retirement accounts.

  One thing to keep in mind here is that opening a brokerage account and only depositing money is not an investment. This is a common mistake a lot of young adults make, believing it is enough. But the final step here is to make a purchase.

- Determine the amount you want to invest – the goals you outline in the first step will help you determine how much you need to invest into each account. You should also check for investment limits depending on the accounts in question.

  Decide on the income percentage you want to invest. The general rule is to invest 15% of your yearly income toward your retirement goals, but depending on your income and your goals, this percentage can vary – as long as you invest a certain amount.

  Also, plan how you want to invest your money. A common question is: Do you want to invest all your money at once or equal amounts of money over time? The answer to this question will lead you to the right investment path.

- Measure your tolerance for risk. I am explaining this a little better below since it is an important step of the process. It basically describes the level of risk you want to take as an investor for the potential of a higher return.

- I mentioned that you are an investor. Think about what kind of investor you want to be – when it comes to investing your money, there is not one approach that will fit everyone. It all depends on your goals, income, savings, knowledge, and willingness to take risks. With that in mind, you can either go for long-term or short-term investing.

  Short-term investing is trading, where you can opt for swing trading or day trading to make an instant profit. It is also the higher-risk option. Long-term investing will never really fall out of style since it gives you time to strategize, allows for a higher margin of error, and allows for more time for compounding interest.

- Develop a solid portfolio – the last step you're about to take in your investing process is to start combining your assets and see which assets will work the best to help you achieve your goals. Some of the most common investments you can add to your portfolio include bonds, mutual funds, stocks, and ETFs.

  As time passes, you want to monitor and rebalance your portfolio if necessary. Doing this allows you to relocate your funds to match your targeted allocation. Carefully follow the market so you won't go into a bad deal and lose money.

Understanding risk and return on investments

This is a trade-off that states how the potential of a bigger return increases when taking a bigger risk. By using this case, many people (not just young adults) associate low-risk levels with low returns and high-risk levels with higher potential returns. To understand this concept, you need to realize that the trading principle connects high risk with high reward. But, here, you should also understand that the people who turn to higher-risk steps have already come to terms with the fact that the investment may not work out.

However, there is some great potential in this, and to fully understand it, you also need to know that, even if some things don't work out with one investment, you can always go to the next one and make a better choice with that – the funds will return to you either way.

Some examples that include measuring singular risk in context include penny stocks and ETFs. For example, the penny stock may have a high risk on a singular basis, but if it only holds one spot in a wide portfolio, then the risk is minimal.

But the core where the risk-return trade-off exists is on a portfolio level. Once you create your portfolio, you will notice it combines risks and returns – some higher, some lower. Now, if you focus on the specific sectors by taking on single positions that represent a larger percentage of holdings, you can increase the risk and reward.

There are a few ways to calculate risk-return. Keep in mind that measuring risk-return investments is quite a complicated subject, and it is not the focus of this book. However, if you want to get started, make use of one of the following ratios below - these are very useful. You always have the possibility to expand your knowledge on that subject if you want to.

Alpha ratio – where you want to check the returns you've earned on an investment above the benchmark return. By using the alpha approach, you measure the excess returns.

Beta ratio – the beta ratio can show you how the stock's correlation stands against the benchmark that determines the overall market. This approach gives a lot of insight whenever you want to do some deeper analysis and check why a certain stock performs more or less in a certain period.

Sharpe ratio – this approach can help you determine if the risk you're taking is worth the reward you might be getting. It is used when you are comparing similar assets in your portfolio. This way, you take into account the degree of risk you might take (or have taken) and check whether it matches (or matched) your gains.

Different investment opportunities suitable for young adults

We're having all this talk about investments, portfolios, stocks, and all that when you are probably confused as they come, and you keep asking yourself one question – how to look for investing opportunities?

The sole idea of investing can be intimidating, especially if you are just starting. But, throughout your life, as you face new and challenging market environments, you look back to this moment and see how it was the perfect time to begin. We talked about risk assessment, so you don't need to jump into some wild rides in the very beginning. You can start as slow and as small as you want – of course, only until you get comfortable. While we are on that subject, let me help you explore some investment options that are suitable for you.

- High-yield savings account – this is probably the simplest way to boost your money return. You can open this account through an online bank, and all you need to know here is that these accounts tend to pay higher interest on average than the standard savings accounts. It is the perfect place to store your saved money and have them hold that for you for a few years, or until an emergency pops up.

- Certificate of deposit – this is another way for you to earn some additional interest on your savings, but in this case, be prepared to have your money tied up longer than you would with the high-yield savings account. If you opt for a certificate of deposit, then you will most likely not be able to touch your money before a certain time is up (this can vary anywhere from 6 months to 5 years or more) without having to pay a fine. That's why this approach is considered to be extremely safe.

- Retirement plan – this plan will benefit you in the future, it is probably one of the simplest ways to begin. You speak to your employer, you match a portion of what you agree to save from your regular paycheck, and that's it. These contributions are made before being taxed and they grow tax-free until you retire.

- Low-cost index funds and ETFs - these are perceived as one of the best beginner-friendly investments. These are designed to track a benchmark index and they don't require any professional expertise or knowledge. They function in a very interesting way - they don't try to beat the market, but rather flow with it and become the market. They are a low-risk investment that would result in a solid long-term return.

Remember the importance of compound interest

Let's continue to a section that can help you build your wealth over time. It is the concept of earning interest on both the interest and the principal amount. Sounds like something you never knew existed, right? Well, in this section, I will explain the basic concept of compound interest and how you can use it to maximize your savings.

Compound interest is a straightforward concept with which you can significantly change your savings. In the long run, it will result in significant growth. Take this as an example – you invest 1k USD at a 10% return, and you will earn 100 USD in interest in the first period. But, if you take that 100 USD and reinvest it, you will earn interest on both – so 10% of the 1k and 10% on the 100. Then, if you take the 110 USD you've made by reinvesting, you can expand the return base. In this case, it will be 10% on the 110, 10% on the 100, and 10% on the 1k. And so on – you can see the pattern here.

Need some help visualizing this in your mind? Here is a table that will make things a lot clearer for you.

Year	Principal	Interest earned	Total amount
1	$1000	$100	$1100
2	$1100	$110	$1210
3	$1210	$121	$1331
4	$1331	$133.1	$1464.1
5	$1464.1	$146.41	$1610.41
10	$2593.74	$259.37	$2853.11
20	$6727.50	$672.75	$7399.25
30	$17449.09	$1744.91	$19194

The compound effect is known by many because it can help you accumulate a significant amount of wealth with little to no effort from your end. Regular investing can help you grow your wealth in the long term.

There is a difference between simple and compound interest. Allow me to explain.

Simple interest is the interest you have earned on the principal amount only. It is mostly used for short-term loans or investments. Compound interest, on the other hand, is used for long-term investments, as you get an interest on your interest, too. It is critical to remain consistent here so you can build up your wealth – think 10, 20, 30 years from now.

So, which strategies can you implement to make this happen?

Start small and start as early as you can. As I mentioned, it is all about consistency because consistency is the principle of taking advantage of the compounding effect. Also, choose the right investment vessel. It is the thing that offers the best compound interest or return, such as stocks that pay dividends.

Constantly reinvest your money rather than taking it out – this way, you will allow for the investments to grow all the time. As previously mentioned, you can always invest in a retirement account, where your investments will grow tax-free until you retire. If you skip this for a few months, your end amount may be significantly lower than expected. Assuming that you miss doing this for a few months, you may lose hundreds of thousands in the end.

I recommend automating your savings and investment contributions. Nowadays, many banks allow this, making it a hassle-free activity that you don't ever have to think about.

Also, try to diversify your investments by utilizing various asset classes, such as real estate, bonds, and stocks, to maximize your long-term returns.

Last but not least – be patient. I know you are a beginner in this field but try not to make an impulsive investment decision based on some short-term fluctuations in the market. Use a compound interest calculator to see the potential impact that interest rates and strategies may have on your financial future.

Before we wrap up this chapter, let's examine another aspect – compound interest and debt. Is this a good combo, and how can you ensure you're on the right road? Compound interest is an excellent way to build wealth, but it can also be a tool that sets you back, especially if you have debt. Credit cards and loans use compound interest to calculate what you owe, and it can lead to a vicious cycle you can't get out of.

For example – you have a credit card with a 20% interest rate yearly and a 1k USD balance. You can only make the minimum payment. This situation will take you over 20 years to pay off the balance, and it will cost you more than 2k in interest charges. The compound interest here makes it more difficult to pay off the debt.

Understanding how compound interest works can help you achieve better financial freedom and independence, especially in the long run. It can also help you make the most of your finances in ways you could not have imagined.

What did you learn from this chapter?

- What is investing?

- The steps you need to take in order to start investing.

- Generally, the higher risk you take, the more it may pay off – and vice versa.

- The starter pack for investment – what are your safest options?

- Compound effect is your golden ticket for long-term wealth growth.

Investing your money, no matter how unknown a terrain may be, is always an exciting one. You get the unique opportunity to learn all about yourself through your portfolio. You learn how to manage and tweak it by keeping a close eye on the market, as well as learning how and when to take risks (that will hopefully pay off in unimaginably good ways). However, it is time to move to some uncharted territory – yet again.

We have come to the part of the book that most people dread. The following chapter is a very important one, so you must not skim through it. It is about taxes – something that every person needs to know about (and pay). Turn the page, and let's go through them together.

CHAPTER 8

THE ONE THING WE ALL HAVE IN COMMON – TAXES

"In this world, nothing can be said to be certain, except death and taxes."

Benjamin Franklin

You are probably familiar with this saying – whether you've heard it from your parents, guardians, teachers, relatives, or a stranger – everybody knows that taxes must be paid.

This may seem a little strange. Instead of congratulating you on your first job, we are here talking about some of its most important aspects (that don't include the actual work). You should pay your taxes no matter what your work or where you live – that means yes, you still need to pay taxes even if you still live with your parents.

Before we begin, here are a few things you need to know:

- Everyone pays taxes all over the world. In the USA, you are required to pay taxes on all income, no matter the source.

That means that you should even submit for income taxes even if you have done some yard work or babysitting.

- The income tax is paid via deduction from your paycheck as you earn it.

- It helps to keep an expense record, as it can help you file an exact annual tax return with the IRS* (this is only in America) before the 15th of April every year. This tax return is based on your income and expenses.

What is the IRS? - IRS is an abbreviation from the Internal Revenue Service. It is an agency based in the U.S. that applies federal tax laws and collects federal taxes from both individuals and companies all across the country. All U.S. citizens are taxpayers, and the tax is paid on an annual level.

Already sounds complicated, doesn't it? Don't worry about it. There is a high probability that your first few tax returns will be very simple, taking into consideration your financial situation. As a young person, you are more likely to have one source of income, and even in this case, there are plenty of ways to minimize the tax you owe.

In this chapter, you will learn all about the implications and how to start early and work early on your taxes. By the end, you will realize that it is easy.

Basics of taxation and their implications on personal finances

Since we are starting from square one, let's answer one question: what are taxes?

Taxes are what you call a "mandatory contribution" to the government entity – this can be local, regional, or national government. We pay taxes because the tax revenues are (most of the time) the primary and sole contributor to any kind of public work – from government activities to building roads and schools and programs such as Medicare.

In the economic world, taxes are the burden that befalls the person who is responsible for them – this can be a person or a business. If we look at this from an accounting perspective, there is a vast array of taxes to consider, some of which include state income taxes, sales taxes, payroll taxes, federal taxes, etc.

Below, you can find some of the most common types of taxes. Learn them, because you should know them!

- Income taxes – giving a percentage of the income you've generated to your state or federal government.

- Payroll taxes – the percentage from the paycheck that the employer withholds from the employee, which is paid to the government on the employee's behalf to fund healthcare and social security programs.

- Corporate taxes – the percentages taken from corporate profits by the government to fund any federal programs.

- Sales taxes – these vary by jurisdiction, but they are levied on specific goods and services.

- Property taxes – depend on the value of the property and the land you own.

- Estate taxes – this is something that applies whenever the property of a person who just died needs to be evaluated, and the total estate has to exceed thresholds that are set by federal and state governments.

- Tariff – also known as taxes on imported goods (added with the belief that it can strengthen domestic business).

The tax system varies greatly from nation to nation, but all of them follow the same rule – everyone needs to pay it. So, before you become a part of the workforce and eligible to pay taxes, you need to study them carefully and know what they're all about. Depending on your current situation, you might even need to pay various taxes.

If we take the USA as an example, how do taxes work exactly? Well, first things first, US taxes are generally known to be lower than in other nations. Only a few years ago, the US tax revenue represented 24% of the Gross Domestic Product (GDP), according to official information, in contrast to other countries, where the average percentage was 34%. In the USA, the taxation increases progressively as your income grows. The tax brackets currently range between 10 and 37 percent, depending on your income.

Okay, now that we have the taxes out of our way, let's talk about taxation. The act of taxation is a term that explains the government imposing a financial obligation on its residents and citizens. You are already aware that people have been paying taxes for a long time now. What the term taxation means is that it applies to all types of mandatory levels, from income taxes to estate taxes.

When you look at it independently, taxation varies from other forms of payment (for example, market exchange) because it is directly connected to any service rendered and does not require consent. However, taxation is not extortion or racket because the imposing institution is the government, not a private entity. Taxation and the formulation of tax policies nowadays are considered to be one of the most critical aspects of modern politics.

History time – taxes in the USA

The American government was originally funded on a very small amount of direct taxation. Instead of that, the federal agencies turned to user fees for government properties. But, when times started getting tough, the government would sell bonds and assets or issue an assessment of the taxes for the rendered services.

The justification for taxation has always been the same. Since the early taxes began, they have been used to raise armies, build defenses, rule classes, and so on. However, as society progressed forward, the justification expanded to economic, utilitarian, and moral considerations. Nowadays, some products and services (for example, gasoline and tobacco) have a higher tax than others. People who have advocated for taxes on public goods theorize that this financial imposition is necessary in case the private provision of public goods is considered to be less than optimal.

At this point in the chapter, you know what taxes are; you know why everyone pays them, but you are still not sure why you're paying them. Here, we go back to the first sentence of this chapter – Benjamin Franklin's words of wisdom. Taxation has been considered the bedrock of modern society since the dawn of time. To live in a society as advanced as the one we have today, we are all paying taxes. You will start paying your taxes so you can enjoy driving the roads, using healthcare, using the public schools, and knowing there is an entire force set in place to protect you (should things ever go wrong). While we, as a society, help the governments fund various undertakings, we can go to bed calmly, knowing that we've done our part in the process of advancing as a whole.

Tax-filing process and common deductions for young adults

We've come to the section where you need to learn how to actually do your taxes. From what you've seen so far from the people around you, it is a hectic process, but once we go through it together, you will realize how simple it is.

Tax filing is something people do every year, and instead of leaving it all to chance and guessing, now we're going to learn how to fill out the annual tax returns.

The tax obligations vary from one individual to the next. Some people may receive a refund on taxes. Others may owe money. That is why you need to know how to complete your taxes correctly from the start and save yourself a headache. Before beginning, you need to check which forms you need with the IRS and verify the deadlines for filing.

The main points you need to explore are:

- Filing status

- Paperwork

- Method

Let's begin.

<u>Filing status</u> – choosing this can help you determine the amount of money you owe, and the different statuses have various tax brackets. If more than one status applies to you, one of them may reduce your tax obligations more than the other one. IRS mainly divides the individuals into the following groups:

- Single – these are all the unmarried taxpayers, including the ones that are legally separated and divorced. The single-filer status also applies to those individuals who do not meet the requirements for head of household status.

- Married filing together – joint filing status means that you are filing the taxes for both incomes combined – your spouse's and yours.

- Married filing individually – those who do not qualify for the joint married filing file their taxes separately. This happens in those cases where spouses prefer to keep their finances separate.

- Head of household – as you can imagine, you can apply for a head of household status if you are single and unmarried with at least one qualifying dependent (a child, a relative such as an older parent, or a sibling with a disability).

- Qualified widow(er) – anyone whose spouse passed away in the year before the current tax year. This taxpayer should also have a child or a stepchild (dependent).

Paperwork – when you're doing your taxes, you need to know how to file all the tax return paperwork correctly. By that, I mean gathering the necessary information and filling it out correctly. Filing taxes correctly means filing a lot of paperwork. You usually receive tax forms for the previous year from your employer, lenders, clients, and financial institutions from January of the current year. There is usually a deadline to file your taxes; in most cases, that deadline is in April. I took the USA as an example here, as this applies there. However, even if I am dissecting the US tax return as an example, that doesn't mean you don't pay taxes if you are in another country - on the contrary. Take a look below at all the forms US citizens use to file their taxes, and which ones are used in which particular cases.

- Income – you need to report your income from every source (remember, this can either be one or multiple sources) using some of the most common income reporting forms. They are:

  - **Form 1040** – This is used to complete your individual tax return.

  - **Form W-2** – This is used to fill out the Wage and Tax Statement – everything made as an employee from an employer, and it also includes taxes withheld, including state, medical, federal, and Social Security taxes.

  - **Form 1099-NEC and 1099-MISC** – Under this category are all non-employee and miscellaneous compensation – from attorneys to freelancers, landlords, and contractors.

  - **Form 1099-INT** – This includes taxes on investment expenses, tax-exempt interest, interest income, withdrawal penalties, and other amounts associated with interest earnings.

  - **Form 1099-DIV** – This records taxes for dividends and distributions.

- Deductions – these can lower your taxable income. You either get a standardized deduction or an itemized deduction. The standardized deduction varies depending on your filing status and the amount you have filed. You can check that to see if you are eligible for a standard deduction. On the other hand, the itemized deduction can be anything where you save receipts and documentation for transactions you want to deduct – such as mortgage interests, extra medical expenses, charitable donations, etc.

- Credits – the deductions may lower your taxable income. Still, the credits can directly reduce your entire tax bill and, with that, completely lower your tax liability (even more than you ever could with a deduction). In the US, some popular tax credits can do this for you:

- Child and dependent care tax credit
- Earned income tax credit
- Premium tax credit
- American Opportunity Tax credit

<u>Method</u> – mainly, there are three ways for you to file your taxes – the method you choose is based on your tax situation and how comfortable you are with filing your taxes.

1. IRS – (again, this is the specific case of the USA) you can file your taxes using Form-1040 with the IRS. Through some partnered websites, you can even file your taxes electronically. There is a step-by-step guide on filing your taxes there, but the fileable forms still require a deeper knowledge of filing taxes. In some countries, the tax officials offer an online platform where you can fill out your tax forms.

2. Software – if you need some help to file your taxes, remember that you don't have to do it alone. Some software programs are incredibly popular nowadays, and they can help you get the correct tax deductions and credits based on your current situation.

3. Tax Professional – knowing how to do taxes is an incredibly valuable skill. If you want to do this right, you can always turn to a professional to help you. That way, you know you can complete your tax return correctly. You don't have to have an account for the entire year; you can only hire an accountant for that particular occasion.

As a young adult, this next bit is exactly what you need – the most common tax deductions. It's important to know what you can deduct as a young adult, so here is the list that will get you started. Here are some of the most common tax deductions:

1. If the employer does not reimburse them – moving expenses.

2. Self-employment tax (as a part of a self-employment taxpayer).

3. Retirement plan contributions as a self-employed individual.

4. Real estate tax.

5. Contributions to charity.

6. Expenses for having an office at home.

7. Tax on any type of vehicle.

8. State and local income taxes.

9. Unreimbursed employee expenses.

10. Student loan interest.

11. Fees and tuition (if you are not claiming an education credit).

12. If you are a homeowner, mortgage interest.

There is also something called tax credits for young adults. In this case, you need to remember that not all tax benefits can qualify as deductions. As a young adult, you can qualify for some tax credits. These include the credits that I mentioned above. Depending on your unique situation, you can check which ones you are eligible for.

There are some things you cannot deduct. No matter how much you try, some things are simply not deductible. These are, for example, personal expenses. So, everything you can think of, such as – clothes, personal grooming, health club, gym membership, groceries, fines, penalties, event tickets, home furnishings – are not deductible. Thankfully, some expenses can still be tax-deducted if you know where to look. Depending on the circumstances, you can dig a little deeper and find these situations. You need to know exactly what you are looking for since this is not always clear-cut. You can get some help from a professional or anyone who has a deeper understanding of the tax law to lend you a hand. Here are a few examples of the exceptions:

- Cell phone – you can get a deduction on your new smartphone. It is not deductible if you get it for your personal use, but it may be deductible if you use it for work or business. It all depends on the facts and circumstances. If you are a self-employed taxpayer and want to get a phone to use for business, then you can deduct the phone. But, if you are an employee and not a business owner, the deduction can only go to the extent that the total exceeds 2% of the taxpayer's gross income.

- Costs for a start-up – you can deduct a few thousand dollars if you are a small business owner.

- Professional expenses and continuing education – naturally, almost all that should be reimbursed by the employer, but if it is not, it can be deducted. But, for example, bar examination fees are not deductible.

- Expenses with a side job – since there are a million ways to enjoy the benefits of a side hustle nowadays, people turn to it the most because any expense that is ordinary and necessary to conduct that business can be deducted. As a taxpayer, remember that information to support your tax file.

- Medical expenses for the elderly – when you pay medical expenses for an elderly parent, you are eligible for a deduction the same way your parents would be eligible for a deduction if you were in each other's place.

- Deduction on clothes – there is still a way you can be eligible for a clothing deduction – if it is required as a condition of employment, and it cannot be adapted for general use as ordinary clothing. The best example is in the case of required uniforms.

Noticing even the smallest details and doing your due diligence can help you reach your goal and claim a deduction on your taxes. Everything you do has its own set of requirements, and some of them can be complex, so always be careful and mindful of the details.

Tips and strategies for minimizing tax liability

Tax liability is the debt or amount of money you owe to the government in taxes as an individual or anyone else. Generally, the term "tax liability" is mostly used to refer to federal income tax liability. In other words, if your income is very low, you won't have any tax liability whatsoever.

How does this apply to you as a young adult?

You can minimize your tax liability by taking a few steps. In this section, I am serving you the best tips and strategies to do that and get the most out of your tax experience. Here's what you can do:

1. Increase your contributions to your retirement – the income tax you pay every year is based on the gross income you have. Gross income is the total amount of money before any credits, taxes, or deductions are accounted for. If you

want to reduce this number, then the best thing you can do is contribute to the employer-sponsored retirement plan or the traditional individual retirement plan – also known as IRA. Suppose the employer plan is not available to you. In that case, you can make contributions with the pre-taxed money, which will directly reduce your taxable income and contribute to your total tax liability in the end.

2. Investment losses turned into profits – this seems a little illogical, but it can be done. If you have some investments that have declined in value since you purchased them, you can sell them – that will reduce your tax liability for the year. This is a very well-known strategy, also known as tax-loss harvesting. In the end, these investment losses will be written off against your investment gains or any other income up to a certain limit every year. Any losses that you cannot take advantage of in the current year – you can carry into your future years and reduce your taxes then.

3. Donating – charities are a great way to reduce your taxes, but only if you itemize deductions on your tax returns and don't go the route of standard deduction. The contribution you make to a qualified charitable organization can be anything from used household items, to goods, or to cash, but keep in mind – any donation that has a value over $250 needs a receipt.

Your tax liability is your tax bill. It may seem like you owe a lot to the government at the beginning, but you can take plenty of steps to minimize that amount. These three steps are the most commonly used ones and the ones you may benefit from the most.

What did you learn from this chapter?

- What are taxes, why everyone needs to pay them, and why are you paying them?

- What taxation means, and why is it used?

- A detailed guide on how to do your taxes.

- The most common deductions for young adults.

- Paying attention to details matters, especially in the case of filing your taxes.

- Not everything can be tax-deducted.

- What is tax liability and how to successfully minimize your tax liability.

There's a very high chance that you have to pay taxes, especially if you have a steady source of income. Any money you've earned from an employer will result in a tax bill. Of course, nobody wants to pay the government more than they should, so this is where learning about taxes comes into the picture.

But as people say, "The storm is behind us," You may not realize it now, but learning all there is to know about taxes will result in you setting sail in the deep financial waters with experience, knowledge, and ease.

It is all about making you feel more confident with money – talking about them, handling them, keeping them, and letting go of them when necessary. The following chapter is one you will hold dear for the rest of your life – as we reach high until we grab your financial independence!

CHAPTER 9

REACH YOUR FINANCIAL INDEPENDENCE

"Money, like emotions, is something you must control to keep your life on the right track."

Natasha Munson.

At the end of the day, financial freedom is something a lot of people dream about. However, actually executing it and becoming financially stable as a young adult takes a lot of courage, knowledge, and persistence. The careful guide you need to create for yourself requires a lot of focus and attention to detail – and that's exactly what we will do in this chapter.

In this final one, I will help you create the best strategies for achieving financial independence as a young adult.

Achieving financial independence at a young age

Being a financially secure person for the rest of your life and achieving that at a young age may sound like a stretch. But, it is not an uncommon practice – a lot of people have done it – the thing is, they don't kiss and tell. So naturally, when you are a young adult struggling to reach financial knowledge and independence, you often feel stuck in a loop you can't get out of. That's understandable because, at the point you're at, you may not have the necessary skills or knowledge to achieve what you want.

That doesn't mean you shouldn't work for it. This book is filled with all kinds of information that will help you become a master of your finances, and these final strategies are the icing on the cake you never knew you needed.

This concept is filled with some remarkably strong strategies that can help you achieve financial security before you even turn 30! No worries. Even if you're a little late to the party, you can still join in!

1. Track how much you spend – the only thing that will keep your spending in check is effectively tracking how much you spend. If you don't want to reach for that pen and paper and write things down – we live in the age of technology! Open your phone and search for any free budgeting app so you can get started.

    Writing down how much you spend is something that can prevent you from wasting the money you've worked so hard to earn. For example, once you see your total bill for all the days you've ordered food instead of making a meal at home, you might rethink deleting that delivery app from your phone.

2. Living within your boundaries – everybody wants something. Everybody wants everything. But of course, not everybody can get everything they want – and for now, neither can you. Take a moment to look through your living standards. Are you spending more than you earn? Do you allow yourself

some expensive goods and services? Can you really afford them, or are you piling up the expenses on multiple credit cards? We've discussed the credit card situation, and now you know it is a bad debt you should get out of as soon as possible. If you want to gain financial independence, you should manage your expectations. Start by reducing your debt and adding more to your savings account. It will do wonders for you both long-term and short-term.

3. Avoid borrowing money – yes, you do have a certain set of standards and a certain lifestyle to maintain, but there is nothing worse than lending money to make it happen. Financial independence doesn't come from borrowing more than you can return. If you want to continue that practice, at least make something of it – invest in yourself. For example, you can invest in your education and your business to get a piece of real estate, etc. In these cases, if you borrow money, it can help you get the leverage you need to reach your financial goals faster than usual. So, it's not about creating a lifestyle you cannot afford, but rather creating something out of it.

4. Short-term goals – one of the best strategies you can implement while you turn your financial life into magic is this one. There are more than just a handful of things that can happen to you as a young adult. Life can throw many curveballs your way, and you won't be able to catch them all. This is when the long-term planning concept comes into the picture. But what about the short-term goals? You can have those set into place, too.

    The best way to start is with a series of short-term goals that are measurable, achievable, and precise. You don't have to do something big – paying off a small debt is the perfect starting point – or saving a certain amount of money in your account. Once you see you can easily do that, you will have a larger chance of achieving your long-term goals. Write down the list of goals and start working toward achieving them!

5. Be financially literate – to make money is sometimes easy – but to know what to do with them can be a challenge for most of you. Thankfully, through all our planning in the previous pages, now you know the area of personal finances that will pay off for the rest of your life. Knowing how to make solid financial and investment decisions is an important strategy that can help you achieve all your financial goals.

6. Save for retirement – since I already mentioned this a few times throughout the book, I cannot stress how important it is. I know that planning for your retirement may be the last thing on your mind at the moment, but if you only take a few steps to make it happen, it will work for you right up to the moment when you blow out the candles on your "Happy Retirement" cake. Even if you decide to save a small amount of money, if you do this early in your life, it will make a difference later on. The contribution plans you make and what we discussed earlier (compound interest) will help you set up a pretty good sum of money for retirement.

7. Don't be afraid to take risks – as long as they are calculated. When you are young, a lot of things can happen – you may get the opportunity to move to a new place, invest in some high-return stocks, take jobs at various companies, and so on. Some things will be a mistake, but some won't. To be on the safer side, you need to take some calculated risks. That way, even if you do make a mistake, you have a lot of time to recover from it. A calculated risk is going back to school for additional training and accepting that job offer that pays more (even though it is in a different city).

8. Keep investing in your biggest asset – you – the thing is, many people turn to the things they want to achieve without looking at themselves first. It is all about paving the way for yourself to move forward, and this can be anything in terms of upgrading your skill set, your knowledge, and your experience. This is a bullet-proof strategy – meaning you will continually upgrade your value in the job market and will keep making smart choices.

   This is a sort of investment that begins in college, and after you've finished it, you should keep upgrading your skills and make sure they are up to date with what the job market needs. It is a lifelong practice but will keep you on the higher-paying end of the workforce.

9. Balance things out – at the end of the day, you are still a young adult – but that doesn't mean you should stop enjoying yourself altogether and focus only on financial stability. It is all about finding the perfect balance between what you spend today and how much you invest for the future. As the last strategy on the list of gaining financial independence early in life, consider it a constant reminder that you should, after all – live. The short-term goals, along with all the other strategies, make up for the perfect plan you can start working on.

The FIRE concept

Understanding the concept of Financial Independence Retire Early, or for short, FIRE, is a movement that revolves around the idea that anyone can achieve financial freedom at a young age. However, this movement takes it to a little bit of an extreme level, where you are supposed to live below your means, save a larger portion of your finances, and invest the saved money into something that will generate a passive income for years to come.

If you want to become a follower of the FIRE plan, then you may be able to retire much earlier than anticipated. However, this approach includes saving up to 70% of your monthly income to your account while still being a full-time part of the workforce. You continue doing that (by living your day-to-day life on the bare minimum) until your savings reach approximately 30 times what you spend in a year (that makes about a million dollars for an average salary). That means you can retire early or quit any form of job employment.

There are more variations to this approach, but the one thing people seem to try out the most is cutting back on their expenses as much as possible. Instead of spending, they put their money aside to invest them – ultimately making the best choice ever. They continue to be an active part of the workforce, but the only alteration they make is – they don't retire that early.

Long-term financial planning and retirement

Have you heard of the term "Failing to plan is planning to fail?" This rings out to be particularly true, especially in the case when you don't make some long-term financial planning or retirement plans. The economic landscape we live in today is quite a complex one. And that is why it is crucial to adopt a more proactive approach. You need to know how to manage your personal finances to the point where you will secure yourself a retirement. In this segment, you are going to learn how to underline the significance of long-term financial planning and retirement, accentuate the risks connected to it, and successfully avoid them.

Let's separate the two so we can focus on one thing at a time.

Long-term financial planning

Let's be honest from the beginning – you are already familiar with what you need to do here, but let's go over the points one more time.

- You need to set a goal – whether it is a short-term or long-term goal, as long as you have it, it can help you create a map that will lead to your financial independence. The goal can be anything you want, from planning a retirement fund to buying a home. It should be a clear and have concise goals that give you the motivation to work for it.

- Manage your cash flow – the cash flow represents everything – your income, savings, expenses, as well as miscellaneous occurrences. Keeping track of it (budgeting it) can help you prevent any overspending and can nudge you in the right direction of the long-term plans you have.

- Manage your debt, too – in fact, make it a priority. If you don't manage your debt properly, then you might hinder your financial progress and jeopardize your long-term plans. Make a repayment plan, prioritize it, and keep as far away as possible from going into more debt.

- Insurance, risk management, the works – this is a vital component of long-term financial planning. It involves assessing any potential risks and adding some insurance coverage so you can mitigate them. Think life insurance, health insurance, disability insurance, and property insurance. These are staples if you want to protect yourself from any unforeseen events that may put a dent in your financial plan.

Retirement planning

There is a specific significance to learning how to make the most out of your retirement plan. Yes, I believe everyone should have one, and instead of worrying about it, all you need to know are a few aspects, most of which we have mentioned before.

- Consider the changing economic landscape – as life expectancy increases, retirement planning has become a very popular choice for a lot of people. Since you might enjoy a longer retirement period, you might want to carefully plan your finances to achieve that.

- Social security considerations – the benefits you may get from your employer can provide you with some financial support in your retirement, but this is often not enough to meet all your expenses. When planning early retirement, you can fill the gap between the retirement income you expect and the lifestyle you desire by adding a lot of additional savings through your retirement accounts and investment vehicles.

  These investment vehicles can be anything from 401(k) plans, other employer-sponsored plans, IRAs (Individual Retirement Accounts), stocks, bonds, mutual funds, and more.

- Consider the ever-changing inflation and healthcare costs – while you save for retirement, keep in mind that you need to factor in the rising healthcare costs and inflation. Retirement is a long-term investment, emphasizing the importance of long-term insurance when you are gradually developing a retirement fund can potentially protect your savings.

Retirements plans in the U.S.

I previously mentioned 401(k) plans and IRAs. Before we conclude this chapter, let's talk about them a little more. Do you know what they are and how can you utilize them? Here is a brief explanation for both of them.

401(k) is also known as an employer-sponsored retirement plan. Employers usually offer the 401(k) and it tends to match the contribution of the employee. The contributions are made before taxes, which means that the total amount of the contributions reduces after being taxed.

With the IRAs, things are different. IRA is an abbreviation for an individual retirement account. If you want to open one, you can do that through a brokerage firm or a bank. Here, you don't have any kind of contribution from an employer.

One thing to keep in mind - you can invest both the 401(k) and the IRA in stocks, securities, and bonds.

So, as you can see, there are many ways you can plan for the future. Your primary plan should always be - investing in yourself and trying to be financially independent and free from a young age. After that, after you've felt like you are standing on solid ground, you can look further into the future - as far as the retirement plans.

What did you learn from this chapter?

- That financial independence at a young age is possible with a lot of planning and determination.

- Some of the best strategies that can help you achieve financial independence.

- What FIRE stands for – a new concept that a lot of people adopt.

- How to focus on long-term financial planning and retirement.

- What is a 401(k) and IRAs?

At the beginning of this chapter, achieving financial freedom and independence as an early adult may have seemed like a very ambitious goal. But after all the possibilities and strategies you discovered here, you can see that it is not impossible to achieve. Everything you want is always within reach. By understanding what you need to do – from setting clear financial goals to investing smartly, exploring multiple income sources, and planning your retirement – you can take the steering wheel and fully control your financial future.

Even if you make some mistakes along the way, holding your balance while you try to achieve your goal is key – and knowing you have the tools and resources to do that just makes things better!

CONCLUSION

"You either master money or, on some level, money masters you."

Tony Robbins

How do you feel now? Do you feel ready to have it all?

Let's briefly review everything you've learned from this book.

The first thing you did was – you learned how to get into the right mindset. Also, you learned there is a specific mindset to get into in the first place. Financial success requires a lot of determination and perseverance, as well as developing a solid perspective. Without it, you will not know which direction to take next. Once you discovered you had some goals, and you brought them onto the surface and wrote them down, you started learning about the compound effect, too. As a concept, this was an eye-opener for you – broadening your horizons to an extent you never knew could be possible.

Then, you realized that your journey would be filled with ups and downs, for you reached the second milestone and immediately started focusing on "what if – the negative version." It is important to know you have the ability to prepare for rainy days, and it costs more to let go of everything and simply go with the flow. You realize you do not want that. The opposite of that kind of behavior is planning, understanding, and managing financial tasks and risks.

With that in mind, the only logical next step was to start setting clear and achievable financial goals – and you managed to execute that beautifully and with ease. The basics of budgeting seem like a piece of cake to you now – what you thought would be quite difficult to overcome was to set and stick to a budget. But, with a few meticulously planned strategies, you discovered there is an easy way to do that, too!

Naturally, before you step into the workforce yourself and exhibit the powerhouse that you are, you learn about debt. This is often a phrase that not a lot of people want to use, talk about, or even think about. But talking and thinking about debt means you have a deeper understanding of the finance subject as a whole. A young adult such as yourself should not be scared by debt but should have the power to differentiate between the good and the bad – which you mastered instantly.

Finally, you reached the point that you were waiting for so long – the book's core and why you picked it up in the first place – how to make money. You have to learn all there is to know about main hustles, side hustles, various job opportunities, and what you need to look for in your unique situation. When exploring multiple income-generating opportunities, you realize what I mentioned in the beginning – this journey will be filled with ups and downs. Balancing multiple income streams with your personal life is as important as the action of making money itself. Now you know how to avoid being in that position where you will only focus on your jobs and nothing else.

Once you start to make money, the only logical next step is to learn how to manage it properly, right? So, I dedicated an entire chapter to investing and laid out a solid plan that could help you multiply your money. As you can see from the chapter, it wasn't anything complicated or difficult. All it took was a little bit of explaining and a few good examples, and you easily got the hang of it.

When you take an active part in the workforce, you must pay taxes. You probably already knew this even before you started reading this book. People talk about taxes all the time – and for a good reason. It is the one thing you absolutely have to do, and the one thing that will stick with you for the rest of your life. Rather than it being a choice, it is an obligation – and the sooner you understand that the better the financial future you will have.

Last but not least, you reached the final chapter of this book, and you learned how to reach financial independence as well! From short-term planning to long-term planning, I managed to cover all the important aspects of finances and gave you the perfect strategies that can help you reach financial independence while you're still a young adult.

Now, with all your newfound knowledge, there is no wonder you have more confidence and are able to approach finances with a smile on your face – you know what you're doing now! It feels like you've inhaled a breath of fresh air, doesn't it? Learning all you've read here usually takes up a lot of time, effort, and energy. But you managed to crash course finances and become literate in a short period of time. I hope that, from this day on, you will take this book as the pillar of your financial knowledge, and you will only upgrade yourself with experience from here on. Finally, you can't wait to get on your financial journey because you already feel like a winner.

One last thing. I still haven't received an answer from you. Are you ready to have it all now?

THANK YOU

Thank you so much for purchasing my book.

The marketplace is filled with dozens and dozens of other similar books but you took a chance and chose this one. And I hope it was well worth it.

So again, THANK YOU for getting this book and for making it all the way to the end.

Before you go, I wanted to ask you for one small favor.

Could you please consider posting a review for my book on the platform? Posting a review is the best and easiest way to support the work of independent authors like me.

Your feedback will help me to keep writing the kind of books that will help you get the results you want. It would mean a lot to me to hear from you.

Leave a Review on Amazon US →

Leave a Review on Amazon UK→

ABOUT THE AUTHOR

Emily Carter is an author who loves helping teens with their biggest turning point in life, adulting. She grew up in New York and is happily married to her high school sweetheart. She also has two of her own children.

In her free time, Emily is an avid volunteer at a local food bank and enjoys hiking, traveling, and reading books on personal development. With over a decade of experience in the education and parenting field she has seen the difference that good parenting and the right tips can make in a teenager's life. She is now an aspiring writer through which she shares her insights and advice on raising happy, healthy, and resilient children, teens, and young adults.

Emily's own struggles with navigating adulthood and overcoming obstacles inspired her to write. She noticed a gap in education regarding teaching essential life skills to teens and young adults. She decided to write comprehensive guides covering everything from money and time management to job searching and communication skills. Emily hopes her book will empower teens and young adults to live their best lives and reach their full potential.

To find more of her books, visit her Amazon Author page at:

https://www.amazon.com/author/emily-carter

REFERENCES

Aspiriant. (13 June 2017). *Making It On Your Own: Taxes*. Aspiriant. https://aspiriant.com/fathom/making-it-on-your-own-taxes/

Baker, B. (13 December 2023). *6 Best Investments For Beginners*. Bankrate. https://www.bankrate.com/investing/best-investments-for-beginners/

Blaine, T. (8 January 2024). *Budgeting For Young Adults: 19 Money Saving Tips For 2024*. Stash. https://www.stash.com/learn/budgeting-for-young-adults/

Boyington, A. (1 June 2023). *How To Do Your Taxes*. Accounting. https://www.accounting.com/resources/how-to-do-taxes/

Carol Dweck: *A Summary Of Growth And Fixed Mindsets*. FS. https://fs.blog/carol-dweck-mindset/

Chen, J. (7 March 2023). *Risk-Return Tradeoff: How The Investment Principle Works*. Investopedia. https://www.investopedia.com/terms/r/riskreturntradeoff.asp

Clear, J. *The Compound Effect By Darren Hardy*. James Clear. https://jamesclear.com/book-summaries/the-compound-effect

Connett, W. (10 July 2022). *10 Steps To Financial Security Before Age 30*. Investopedia. https://www.investopedia.com/articles/younginvestors/08/generation-y.asp

Cruze, R. (29 December 2023). *How To Set Financial Goals: 6 Steps*. Ramsey Solutions. https://www.ramseysolutions.com/personal-growth/setting-financial-goals

Debt.com. (10 January 2923). *Good Debt Vs Bad Debt*. LinkedIn. https://www.linkedin.com/pulse/good-debt-vs-bad-debt-com/

Fontinelle, A. (14 March 2024). *8 Financial Tips For Young Adults*. Investopedia. https://www.investopedia.com/articles/younginvestors/08/eight-tips.asp

GFOA. (4 March 2022). *Long-Term Financial Planning*. GFOA. https://www.gfoa.org/materials/long-term-financial-planning

Gorton, D. (22 December 2023). *Taxes Definition: Types, Who Pays, And Why*. Investopedia. https://www.investopedia.com/terms/t/taxes.asp

Heger, E. (24 February 2024). *Personal Finance 101: Budgeting Basics*. Synchrony. https://www.synchronybank.com/blog/budgeting-basics/

Horton, M. (5 March 2024). *What Are Some Ways To Minimize Tax Liability?* Investopedia. https://www.investopedia.com/ask/answers/040715/what-are-some-ways-minimize-tax-liability.asp

Izad, S. (31 May 2023). *The Importance Of Financial Planning And Retirement Planning: Failing To Plan Is Planning To Fail*. LinkedIn. https://www.linkedin.com/pulse/importance-financial-planning-retirement-failing-plan-sam-izad/

Kagan, J. (28 February 2024). *Taxation Defined, With Justifications And Types Of Taxes*. Investopedia. https://www.investopedia.com/terms/t/taxation.asp

Kerr, A. (29 February 2024). *Financial Independence, Retire Early (FIRE) Explained: How It Works*. Investopedia. https://www.investopedia.com/terms/f/financial-independence-retire-early-fire.asp

Longgrear, J. (4 May 2023). *How To Manage Work-Life Balance With Multiple Income Streams*. Fast Company. https://www.fastcompany.com/90874827/how-to-manage-work-life-balance-with-multiple-income-streams

Matthews, K. (16 January 2024). *A Beginner's Guide To Investing In The Stock Market*. Fortune Recommends. https://fortune.com/recommends/investing/how-to-start-investing/

Modi, P. (19 December 2023). *The Importance Of Exploring Diverse Income Streams Early In Life*. Education Next. https://www.educationnext.in/posts/the-importance-of-exploring-diverse-income-streams-early-in-life

Mukherji, S. (27 August 2023). *The Ultimate Guide: How To Achieve Financial Freedom Before 30*. LinkedIn. https://www.linkedin.com/pulse/ultimate-guide-how-achieve-financial-freedom-before-30-sujoy-mukherji/

PowHERhouse Money Coaching. (13 March 2023). *5 Tips To Manage Student Debt*. LinkedIn. https://www.linkedin.com/pulse/5-tips-manage-student-debt-powherhouse-money-coaching/

See, B. (31 March 2023). *The Side Hustles 2023: Exploring The Growing Trend Of Independent Work*. LinkedIn. https://www.linkedin.com/pulse/side-hustles-2023-exploring-growing-trend-independent-bobby-see/

Sharma, V. (14 April 2023). *The Magic Of Compounding – Making Money Work For You*. LinkedIn. https://www.linkedin.com/pulse/magic-compounding-making-money-work-you-vaibhav-sharma/

SJB Global. (13 December 2023). *Financial Mindset*. SJB Global. https://sjb-global.com/financial-mindset/

Slifka, R. (6 November 2023). *15 Quotes About Finance From Money-Saving Experts*. Chime Money Moves. https://www.chime.com/blog/15-quotes-from-our-favorite-money-saving-experts/

Tax Deductions And Credits For Young Adults. H&R Block. https://www.hrblock.com/tax-center/filing/adjustments-and-deductions/tax-deductions-for-young-adults/

Taxes Quotes. Brainy Quote. https://www.brainyquote.com/topics/taxes-quotes

Understanding Risk Management In Finance. AccountsIQ. https://www.accountsiq.com/accounting-glossary/understanding-risk-management-in-finance/

Verma, E. (5 March 2024). *What Is Financial Risk And Its Types? Everything You Need To Know*. Simplilearn. https://www.simplilearn.com/financial-risk-and-types-rar131-article

Wealthwrite Company. (20 October 2023). *Role Of Emergency Funds In Financial Security*. LinkedIn. https://www.linkedin.com/pulse/role-emergency-funds-financial-security-wealthwrite-company-msmwc/

What Are The Best Practices For Developing A Long-Term Financial Plan? LinkedIn. https://www.linkedin.com/advice/0/what-best-practices-developing-long-term-financial-nmp9f

Yu, J. (26 February 2024). *5 Basic Methods For Risk Management.* Investopedia. https://www.investopedia.com/articles/investing-strategy/082816/methods-handling-risk-quick-guide.asp